CW00730354

haydée santamaría rebel lives **haydée santamaría**

cover photo: Haydée Santamaría, right, with Celia Sánchez,
in the Sierra Maestra mountains, Cuba, 1958

also published in the **rebel lives** series:

Helen Keller, *edited by John Davis*
Albert Einstein, *edited by Jim Green*

forthcoming in the **rebel lives** series:

Sacco & Vanzetti, *edited by John Davis*
Louise Michel, *edited by Nic Maclellan*
Tamara "Tania" Bunke, *by Ulises Estrada*

rebel lives, a fresh new series of inexpensive, accessible and provocative books unearthing the rebel histories of some familiar figures and introducing some lesser-known rebels

rebel lives, selections of writings by and about remarkable women and men whose radicalism has been concealed or forgotten. Edited and introduced by activists and researchers around the world, the series presents stirring accounts of race, class and gender rebellion

rebel lives, does not seek to canonize its subjects as perfect political models, visionaries or martyrs but to make available the ideas and stories of imperfect revolutionary human beings to a new generation of readers and aspiring rebels

haydée santamaría

edited by Betsy Maclean

Ocean Press
Melbourne ■ New York
www.oceanbooks.com.au

Published in association with the Casa de las Américas

Cover design by Sean Walsh and Meaghan Barbuto

Copyright © 2003 Ocean Press
Copyright © 2003 Casa de las Américas

All rights reserved. No part of this publication may be reproduced, stored in a retrieval system or transmitted in any form or by any means, electronic, mechanical, photocopying, recording or otherwise, without the prior permission of the publisher.

ISBN: 1-876175-59-1

Library of Congress Catalog Card No: 2003106570
First Printed in Australia 2003

Published by Ocean Press

Australia: GPO Box 3279, Melbourne, Victoria 3001, Australia
                Fax: (61-3) 9329 5040 Tel: (61-3) 9326 4280
                E-mail: info@oceanbooks.com.au

USA: PO Box 1186, Old Chelsea Stn., New York, NY 10113-1186, USA
                Tel: (1-718) 246 4160

Ocean Press Distributors:

United States and Canada: **Consortium Book Sales and Distribution**
        Tel: 1-800-283-3572   www.cbsd.com

Britain and Europe: **Global Book Marketing**
        E-mail: orders@globalbookmarketing.co.uk

Australia and New Zealand: **Palgrave Macmillan**
        E-mail: customer.service@macmillan.com.au

Cuba and Latin America: **Ocean Press**
        E-mail: oceanhav@enet.cu

www.oceanbooks.com.au

contents

dedication

Very much a collaborative effort, this book is the product of much love and many voices. My thanks especially to the Santamaría family, Javier Salado, Ligia Trujillo, the Casa de las Américas and the Ocean Press crew for their support and invaluable insights on their beloved Haydée. Blessed with a revolutionary family of my own, the input of David Maclean, Kofi Taha, Catherine Murphy, Karen Oh and my heart, Eric Miles, was — and continues to be — essential in this and other transformative projects.

This book is dedicated to the spirit of Haydée Santamaría, alive and well in the lives and work of Josefina Bocourt Díaz and Teresa Rimada Reyes, my personal connection to the ordinary extraordinariness that is Cuba.

BM

chronology

1922 Haydée Santamaría is born to Joaquina Cuadrado and Abel Benigno Santamaría.

Early 1950s Haydée Santamaría and her brother Abel move to Havana from Encrucijida in central Cuba.

March 10, 1952 Fulgencio Batista overthrows the democratically elected government of Carlos Prío Socorras.

1952-53 Haydee and Abel meet Fidel Castro and begin organizing the attack on the Moncada Garrison.

July 26, 1953 The Moncada Garrison attack, in which 160 rebels attack the military barracks in Santiago de Cuba. Most are killed. Haydée and Melba Hernández are among those captured. Haydée's brother Abel, and her fiancé Boris Luis Santa Coloma, are among those tortured and killed. Fidel Castro escapes, only to be captured a few days later and put on trial with some 27 additional combatants.

October 1953 The trial of the Moncada combatants. Fidel Castro makes his famous *History Will Absolve Me* speech.

May 1954 Haydée and Melba are released from prison. They organize the printing and circulation of *History Will Absolve Me*.

June 1955 Fidel Castro is released from prison, after an intensive popular campaign. Around this time, the July 26 Movement is formed.

July 7, 1955 Fidel Castro arrives in Mexico with the goal of organizing an armed expedition to Cuba. He meets Che Guevara there.

1956 Haydée marries Armando Hart, future minister of education.

November 30, 1956 Urban uprising in Santiago de Cuba, led by Frank País, Haydée and Celia Sánchez. The July 26 Movement organizes an urban rebellion to coincide with the scheduled arrival of the *Granma*. Soundly defeated by Batista's police, a wave of arrests and assassinations soon follows.

December 2, 1956 *Granma* landing. The yacht carrying Fidel and the rebel troops arrives from Mexico at Las Coloradas in Oriente Province, two days late due to inclement weather.

July 30, 1957 Frank País is murdered by Batista henchmen in Santiago de Cuba.

September 4, 1958 The Mariana Grajales platoon, comprising only women fighters, is formed in the Sierra Maestra.

1958 Haydée is sent abroad to organize for the July 26 Movement in Miami, Florida.

January 1, 1959 Triumph of the revolution. Batista flees the country.

January 2, 1959 Haydée returns to Cuba.

January 8, 1959 Fidel Castro and his Rebel Army march into Havana.

1959 The Casa de las Américas is created; Haydee is named director.

January 3, 1961 The United States officially breaks off diplomatic relations with Cuba and implements the economic embargo and travel ban that still exist today.

1961 The Cuban Literacy Campaign. Almost 400,000 students and teachers volunteer to teach rural peasants how to read. Within one year Cuba's illiteracy rate is reduced to less than four percent.

April 17, 1961 Bay of Pigs invasion, in which Cuban exiles, trained, armed and funded by the CIA, invade Cuba at the Bay of Pigs (Playa Girón). After three days of fighting, the invading force is defeated by the Cuban Army.

April 19, 1961 Fidel Castro formally declares the socialist character of the revolution.

October 1962 The Cuban Missile Crisis begins when U.S. reconnaissance aircraft photograph the Soviet construction of intermediate-range missile sites in Cuba.

1960s Silvio Rodríguez, Pablo Milanés and other members of the Nueva Trova movement perform at Casa de las Américas, with Haydée's support.

October 3, 1965 Central Committee of the Communist Party of Cuba is created. Haydée is among its members.

1967 Haydée presides over the Latin American Organization for Solidarity Conference (OLAS), held in Havana.

October 9, 1967 Che Guevara is killed in Bolivia by U.S.-trained soldiers in the village of Vallegrande, Bolivia.

1968 Haydée travels to Vietnam as part of a solidarity delegation.

September 11, 1973 Chilean President Salvador Allende is overthrown in a CIA-orchestrated military coup.

January 1980 Celia Sánchez, Haydée's dear friend and revolutionary heroine, dies of cancer.

July 28, 1980 Haydée Santamaría Cuadrado dies.

"There is a moment when all things can be beautiful, heroic. That moment when life defies death and defeat, because one holds on to it, because it's so important not to lose it. At such a moment, one risks everything to preserve what really counts. Life and death can be beautiful, and noble, when you fight for your life, but also when you give it up without compromise. All I have wanted to show our young Cubans is that life is more beautiful when you live that way. It is the only way to live."

—*Haydée Santamaría*

introduction

"Our worldly happiness could very well have begun in a small apartment, on a small island, on our small planet; and now it is our turn to take care of the sun."

Haydée Santamaría's words perfectly describe the world which she, and all revolutionaries, inhabit: that space between dreams and reality, between particularity and possibility. One of Latin America's most inspiring 20th century women revolutionaries, Haydée's persistent courage and endless commitment to social justice blazed a trail for generations of *guerrilleras* to come. But it was her almost singular dedication to internationalism that set her apart. Her legacy is not only that of a woman who bravely fought for the liberation of her country but also that of a revolutionary whose heart and mind knew not national boundaries or ideological limitations.

Outside of her own revolutionary Cuba, outside of the Casa de las Américas' Latin American cultural circle, however, the story of Haydée Santamaría is not well known. Though she was one of only two women who fought in the July 26, 1953, attack on the Moncada Garrison in Santiago de Cuba — the battle that marked the beginning of the Cuban Revolution that triumphed in 1959 and has endured against all odds to date — her picture is not emblazoned on T-shirts or dorm room posters, her revolutionary insights are not quoted in feminist journals or revolutionary tracts. You find her instead in the small places: in the vivid memories of women who fought with her in the urban underground; in the warm smiles of writers, dancers, painters and musicians who recall her steadfast support and explosive sense of humor; in the names of young girls throughout the Americas whose mothers, so moved by her example, named their own Haydées in her honor.

Why has this giant of revolutionary history, this shining example of feminism and internationalism, been relegated to the shadowy corners of Latin American political memory? The reasons are as numerous and as complex as history itself, but at least three warrant a closer look. First, Haydée's own humility shunned the spotlight: she fulfilled her role in the Cuban Revolution as her duty to humanity, not for fame nor for glory but, in her own words, "to take care of the sun." Second, there is the obvious sexism plaguing all history — revolutionary or not — that habitually renders the contributions of women invisible. Finally, the circumstances of Haydée's death may have most clouded the celebration of her life. For at the same moment in which she secured her place in history, the loss of her beloved brother, her lover and some 70 fellow combatants condemned her to death. Twenty-seven years and two days after the bloody attack on the Moncada, Haydée Santamaría did what revolutionaries are not supposed to do: she laid down her revolutionary armor and took her own life.

Much time has been spent wondering why Haydée committed suicide. Cuba detractors suggest that Haydée was sickened by Cuba's strengthening alliance with the Soviet Union, that she felt betrayed by Fidel Castro's foray into socialism. Any serious contemplation of her life and work will quickly dismiss such notions. More credible accounts maintain that it was the death earlier that year of her close friend Celia Sánchez — Fidel's most trusted aide and the fourth of the quartet of Cuban revolutionary women that includes Haydée, her fellow Moncada combatant Melba Hernández, and Federation of Cuban Women head Vilma Espín. Many claim that Haydée never truly recovered from her brother Abel's tortuous death, after the Moncada attack, at the hands of Batista's henchmen. There was also her failing health after a near fatal car accident months before, which left her in constant pain. The truth, of course, is that we will never know exactly why Haydée chose to end her own life. But we can intimate the depths of her grief by listening to her own words. As far back as 1967, following Ernesto Che Guevara's death in Bolivia, Haydée wrote the following in a farewell letter to her beloved friend and revolutionary collaborator:

> Fourteen years ago I witnessed the death of human beings so immensely loved that today I feel tired of living; I think I have lived too much already. I do not see the sun as so beautiful, I do not feel pleasure in seeing the palm trees. Sometimes, like now, despite enjoying life so much and realizing that it is worthwhile to open one's eyes every morning if only for those two things, I feel like keeping them closed, like you.

Haydée's story reminds us that a revolutionary's life is filled not only with the great joy of ideological commitment, but, more often than not, with tremendous, almost overwhelming pain. The massacre and subsequent torture of the July 26 militants at Moncada signaled only the beginning of the loss that Haydée would endure. Abel, her brother; Boris, her fiancé; Frank País, the young and exemplary leader of the urban underground; Che, whose death so profoundly affected not only Cuba but the world; and finally Celia — these names make up the short list of Haydée's loved ones lost to the revolution. The cause of her grief then, is clear. Less apparent is not what led to her death, but what kept her alive.

The second of five children, Haydée was born on a sugar plantation in central Cuba in 1922. Her parents, Abel Benigno and Joaquina, were small-time landowners of Spanish descent.

In the early 1950s Haydée, 26 years old, came to Havana with her younger brother Abel, 22, in order to keep an eye on him. Long identifying with the oppressed — from the baby chickens on her family farm to the Cuban independence heroes, the Mambís — Haydée's sympathy for the growing student movement against government corruption came quickly and easily. And so it was that when Abel brought a young and fiery Fidel Castro home one day, the two young insurgents found both an open heart and a revolutionary spirit in Haydée.

It was that now famous apartment in Havana which saw the beginnings of what was to become the July 26 Movement — the movement that eventually overthrew the dictator Fulgencio Batista and constructed the Cuban Revolution from the ground up. Well aware of their siblings' political involvement, Aldo and Aida, two of the remaining Santamaría children, sat out of the Moncada attack in order to protect their aging parents. By the end of the revolution, however, the entire Santamaría clan was involved in the struggle in one form or another, most especially Haydée's brother Aldo, who was arrested on a number of occasions, and her mother Joaquina.

Much has been written about the [1953] attack on the Moncada Garrison, in fact, an entire book dedicated to Haydée's remembrances of that fateful day will be published by Ocean Press in an expanded edition that includes a prologue by Celia María Hart, Haydée Santamaría's daughter. Suffice to say that Haydée showed tremendous courage and extraordinary vision during the operation. Her objective, long after the attack had fallen apart, was to continue fighting long enough to allow for Fidel's escape. This proved to have been a crucial decision. Batista's troops responded quickly and brutally to the assault — killing or capturing and subsequently torturing and murdering almost three-quarters of the young insurgents. Fidel escaped while Haydée and Abel were among those captured. It was in their adjoining cells that Haydée's fate was sealed — as both a revolutionary hero and a woman tortured by loss. It is worth quoting extensively Fidel's recounting of Haydée's story, made famous in his courtroom defense, *History Will Absolve Me*:

> A sergeant, with several other men, came with a bleeding human eye in his hand into the cell where our comrades Melba Hernández and Haydée Santamaría were held. Addressing the latter, and showing her the eye, they said: "This eye belonged to your brother. If you will not tell us what he refused to say, we will tear out the other." She, who loved her brave brother above all other things, replied with dignity: "If you tore out an eye and he did not speak, neither will I." Later they came back and burned their arms with cigarette butts until at last, filled with spite, they told young Haydée Santamaría: "You no longer have a boyfriend, because we killed him too." And, still imperturbable, she answered: "He is not dead, because to die for one's homeland is to live forever." Never before has the heroism and the dignity of Cuban women reached such heights.

There are, of course, other stories, less brutal and perhaps more telling, surrounding the legendary history of Haydée Santamaría. There is the story of Haydée's train trip to Santiago weighed down with a suitcase filled with weapons. As she was getting on the train, a soldier offered to help her with her luggage. Shocked by the incredible weight of the bag, he asked what on earth she could be carrying. Calm and collected in what seemed to be any situation, this shy girl from the countryside somehow convinced that soldier that she was on her way back to university, with a suitcase full of books. Her July 26 *compañeros* thought they had surely been found out when they saw Haydée stepping down from her compartment with the very same soldier at her side, carrying their precious cargo. Instead, the soldier walked up to the patiently waiting militants, dropped the suitcase at their feet and with a squeeze of his hand and a wink, Haydée sent him on his way.

And so Haydée passed the war as a gunrunner, tactician, international fundraiser, coordinator of the urban underground and guerrilla combatant. The triumph of the revolution in January 1959 brought with it a host of well-known international consequences. Deeply embedded in a global context fueled by the Cold War, Cuba's choice to pursue a socialist path prompted swift political and economic isolation. With visionary insight, Haydée identified what she believed was the one crack in the ideological blockade being built around her island — culture. That realization gave birth to the Casa de las Américas, which evolved into the foremost cultural institution in all of Latin America. With her internationalist vision in tow, Haydée transformed herself from *guerrillera* to cultural emissary, choosing to wield art and culture as powerful weapons for social change.

Casa was created in 1959. Under Haydée's direction, Casa set before itself the Herculean task of "affirmation, defense and promotion of the values of what Cuban patriot and revolutionary José Martí called 'Our America,'" and, by most accounts, Casa succeeded in doing just that. Through the years Casa hosted and published Latin American cultural giants, from Gabriel García Márquez, Pablo Neruda and Marta Conti to José Saramago, Alicia Alonso and Eduardo Galeano.

The institution that Haydée built published numerous books by Latin America's greats whose controversial words may have remained otherwise unpublished in the culture of artistic repression sweeping the continent in the 1960s and 1970s. In addition, Casa printed its own political-literary magazine, edited by Roberto Fernández Retamar, renowned Cuban poet, writer and Haydée's constant companion at Casa, whose words about his beloved mentor and collaborator are included in this collection. Casa was also responsible for bringing some of the world's most celebrated dancers, musicians, painters and theater groups to the island as part of the revolutionary imperative to rectify decades of cultural elitism and bring art to the Cuban people. Home to one of Latin

America's most extensive art collections, Casa also gathered some of Latin America's most important literary works in its library. Finally, and representative of Haydée's own revolutionary imperative, Casa became a kind of home away from home, a refuge for artists of all genres fleeing persecution in their own countries.

Eminent Uruguayan poet Mario Benedetti himself sought refuge at Casa during the worst years of repression under Uruguay's military dictatorship. When he finally was able to return to his homeland, after years of close collaboration with Haydée, it was her internationalism that most impressed this literary mastermind:

> For painters, musicians, writers, singers, theater people from Argentina or Venezuela, from Chile or Mexico, from Uruguay or Nicaragua, from Jamaica or El Salvador, and of course in her native Cuba, the very mention of Haydée Santamaría signifies a world, an attitude, a sensibility, and also a revolution, which she did not conceive of as confined to the land of José Martí, but extended to the future of all our peoples.

It was in their internationalism that Che and Haydée met and overlapped. It has been said that together, the two of them "brought Latin America to Cuba." Neither Che nor Haydée were satisfied with the liberation of Cuba because theirs was not a battle against a tyrant but against tyranny. Theirs was the struggle for humanity, for justice in its most profound and expansive expression.

Even within the revolution of her making, Haydée continued to challenge limitations, boundaries both national and intellectual. Despite her membership in the pantheon of Cuban revolutionary heroes, Haydée refused to become an anachronism. One well-known example of her resoluteness was her steadfast defense of Silvio Rodríguez and Pablo Milanés, now two of Cuba's most famous sons, when their Nueva Trova [New Song] movement first appeared on Cuba's musical scene. During a time of ideological retrenchment, their political lyrics and challenging stance were frequent targets for attack from doctrinaire Cuban bureaucrats. Haydée shielded the talented young singers and cautioned against dogmatism in all of its forms. "Remember," she regularly counseled international jurists upon their arrival in Cuba for the Casa competition, "don't worry too much about awarding works that are politically impeccable; just concern yourselves with giving the prize to the best." Due to her untiring support and encouragement, Haydée was largely credited for creating the atmosphere that spawned the rich and globally celebrated cultural contributions by Cuban artists during the 1960s, 1970s and 1980s. Without question, highly innovative and influential art continues to flow from the tiny island nation to this day.

Haydée speaks to us then, on many levels: as a revolutionary, a feminist, an internationalist — but more than anything, she speaks to us as Haydée, Yeyé to her close friends and family. There is a Cuban saying, *"Cuando lo extraordinario se vuelve cotidiano hay la revolución,"* which, loosely translated, declares: "When the extraordinary becomes ordinary, that is the revolution." Haydée Santamaría embodies this sense of greatness expected, of the remarkable turned probable. It is hard to imagine what makes such a fundamental transformation possible, but one glimpses it in the streets of Havana, in an expansive way of being which seems to recognize membership in — and responsibility to — a larger community. To foreign eyes, it is hard to pin down what makes Cuba feel so different, harder still to trust that it is real. Haydée not only knew what it was but sought it out, and, eventually exemplified it — this elusive ordinary extraordinariness that makes a revolution.

This book is made up of works by Haydée herself, her thoughts on the Moncada attack, on the formation of the Casa de las Américas, on her friend and *compañero* Che and on revolutionary internationalism. It also includes work about Haydée: letters, essays, poems and eulogies by some of Latin America's most celebrated artists and political activists, all written on the occasion of her death. Included are remembrances by those who knew Haydée best: Roberto Fernández Retamar, himself a brilliant writer and two-time winner of the Cuban National Prize for Literature, who worked at Haydée's side through the formation of Casa and has stood at its helm since her death; Melba Hernández, Haydée's constant revolutionary companion at Moncada, throughout their subsequent prison term and in the revolutionary struggle both before and after the triumph of the revolution; Silvio Rodríguez, Cuba's own Bob Dylan, a Latin American troubador and politically poetic songwriter who has performed for adoring crowds of hundreds of thousands throughout Latin America; Alicia Alonso, Cuba's prima ballerina and the soul of Havana's National Theater; and of course, Fidel Castro, the architect of the Cuban Revolution and a fundamental presence in Haydée's life. Also included are contributions from Latin America's finest poets, painters and political commentators, including Costa Rican poet and essayist Carmen Naranjo; Alejandro Obregón, Colombian painter, muralist, sculptor and engraver and winner of the Guggenheim prize; and Chilean writer and Duke University professor of Literature and Latin American Studies, Ariel Dorfman, whose astute commentary on everything from Augusto Pinochet to Disneyland have won him international acclaim.

These selections were made painstakingly from a mountain of possibilities which, if included in their entirety, would easily fill a book at least three times this size. The sheer quantity and remarkable quality of the tributes stockpiled in the Casa de las Américas library speaks volumes for a woman well-loved, tremendously respected and deeply missed.

In the end death found Haydée not in a Bolivian valley, in the Chilean presidential palace, on the battlefields of Nicaragua, nor on the dais in a Harlem ballroom. On that July day, Haydée Santamaría died as extraordinary women pass from our world, not in a blaze of glory, but in a quiet room, in love and in pain. She knew only too well José Martí's words when he said, "A good soul on earth hurts very much." But as Melba Hernández reminds us, "Yeyé is not dead, she is alive and will live on eternally in all those who know that happiness is only found when we give ourselves to the great work that is on behalf of the peoples, on behalf of humanity."

Thus, as sure as she found the spirit of Che among the "Bolivian miner... Peruvian mother... the guerrilla that is or is not but will be," we will find Haydée today in the Lacandon jungle, the Brazilian favela, the Palestinian refugee camp. So as the nation that knew her so well celebrates her extraordinary contributions, it is time for the world to reclaim this revolutionary heroine. And let us love and learn from her not in spite of her death, but because of her existence as an exceptional being — a complete, complex human being — who both lived and died committed to justice for all peoples.

Betsy Maclean
Brooklyn, USA • May 2003

part one: *fire*

By Haydée

A Personal Account of the Moncada

Haydée Santamaría

In this piece, Haydée recounts with vivid detail a few powerful moments of the Moncada Garrison attack. She relives her revolutionary conviction throughout the battle and her devastation at the sight of so many compañeros, *including her beloved brother Abel, who were killed that bloody July morning.*

Melba [Hernández] is the one who remembers everything with the greatest accuracy. I no longer remember precise times, and maybe she doesn't either, after so many things and so many years. But before, when we got around to talking of those times, she found it easier to recall events in detail.

If I start to talk and keep talking about the Moncada [attack in 1953], I'm sure I will remember many things.

What I most reflect on now is about those of us who went to the Moncada and I ask myself: "Fidel being how he is, how is it possible that anyone could have betrayed him? How is it possible that they didn't understand him? How is it possible that not all of us were perfectly identified with Fidel, with the revolution?"

Every time I see Fidel, speak with him, hear him on television, I think of the other boys, all those who died and all of those who are still alive, and I think of Fidel, the Fidel we knew back then and the Fidel who is still the same today. I think of the revolution that is still the same one we took to the Moncada.

Melba, Abel, Renato, Elpidio and I were in the Siboney farmhouse. Renato decided to make chicken with tomatoes and peppers. I laughed when he told me and began to argue that it really was a fricassee. "That's what they call it in Vuelta Abajo," Renato insisted.

While we were cooking and talking with Melba and Renato, I was looking at Abel and thinking of the last time we were at the sugar mill (in Encrucijada) to say goodbye to our parents and family. When we were about to leave the house in the early hours of the morning to return to Havana, Aida asked us to take care not to wake the baby. Abel wanted to pick her up and give her a kiss.

I said: "Let's go, maybe it's the last time we'll see her."

Aida looked at me in alarm, and I wanted to make a joke: "We'll probably get killed on the highway."

"Don't be so tragic," Aida said to me, and we left.

When Renato's "chicken with tomatoes and peppers" was done, Abel didn't want to eat. He was going to Santiago with an elderly couple who lived across the way from the Siboney farmhouse. "Perhaps it will be the last Carnival they see," I thought.

Melba was at my side, we hadn't been apart for a single day in seven months. I was thinking about the house, about Melba, about the boys. At that time, it hadn't occurred to me to think about death, but there were two things that filled me with pain. If everything failed and Fidel was lost, we would make the revolution for him and our lives and actions would have meaning; the other came to me much later, with a terrible agony, when our dead were lying amongst blood and earth and we knew that we wouldn't see them any more: I feared that I would be separated from Melba. I remember Melba trying to protect me; me trying to protect her and both of us trying to protect each other, in everything we did, whenever other lives were in danger. Anything could have happened under the bullets, under the bursts of the machine guns, among the cries of pain of those who fell wounded, among the last moans of those who were dying. Anything is both a little and a lot, and nobody knows how an action of that nature is going to turn out. Nobody knows what's going to happen in the minutes that follow. There are things that one knows, like everything that one loves. I went to the Moncada with the people I most loved. Abel and Boris were there, Melba was there and Fidel and Renato and Elpidio and the poet Raúl were all there, along with Mario and Renato and Chenard and the other boys. Cuba was at stake, the dignity of our offended people and their violated freedom, and the revolution that would return people's destiny to their own hands.

The boys arrived hungry. Midnight found us talking, laughing, all of us cracking up and telling jokes. We served up coffee and a little of the food that was left, what Abel hadn't eaten. We reverted to telling stories, the anecdote of my arrival in Santiago with two suitcases full of weapons and obviously heavy, so much so that a soldier in the same carriage who lifted them asked if they contained dynamite. "Books," I told him, "I've just graduated and I'm going to Santiago, to take advantage of Carnival and enjoy myself a bit after studying. You'd make a good partner to enjoy myself with at Carnival." The soldier smiled amicably and told me where we should meet. He got down on the platform with me, carrying my case. Abel and Renato were waiting for me in the terminal. I got close enough to tell them: "That's the case," and added: "This is a friend from the journey." And to the soldier: "These are two friends who have come to meet me." The soldier handed over the case and we left.

One of the boys was joking with Boris, my fiancé.

"Watch out for Yeyé, she's got a date in the dark with a soldier of the dictatorship," and we all laughed.

Then Fidel arrived and then we all left, some of us individually, and others in a group.

Soon after, Melba, Gómez García, Mario Muñoz and I were in the car. After and during the journey to the Moncada I thought about home, I thought of the morning that was approaching: "What was going to happen? What would they say at home? How would the day that was just beginning turn out?"

And then we arrived at the Moncada.

Then the first seconds went by and the first minutes and then the first hours — the worst, bloodiest, cruelest, most violent moments of our lives. They were the hours in which everything can be heroic and valiant and sacred. Life and death can be noble and beautiful and one has to defend life or give oneself up to it completely.

These are the facts that Melba recalls exactly. Those that I have tried unsuccessfully to forget. Those that I remember are enveloped in a cloud of blood and smoke, those that I shared with Melba, those that Fidel narrates in *History Will Absolve Me*: the death of Boris and of Abel. Death mowing down the boys that we loved so much, death staining the walls and the grass with blood. Death dominating everything, conquering everything. Death imposing itself like a necessity. And the fear of living after so many deaths and the fear of dying before those who had to die had died and the fear of dying when life could still win the final battle over death.

There are those moments during which nothing can shock you, neither death, the bursts of machine gun fire, the smoke, the smell of burnt, bloodied and dirtied flesh, nor the smell of warm blood, nor the smell of cold blood, nor blood on one's hands, nor flesh ripped into pieces, coming apart in one's hands, nor the moans of those dying. Nor the terrifying silence in the eyes of those who have died. Nor the semi-parted lips on which it seems that there is a word that, if spoken, would freeze your soul.

There is that moment at which everything can be beautiful and heroic. That moment at which life, however much it means and however important, challenges and conquers death. And you feel your hands clutching a wounded body that is not the body we loved, which could be the body of one of those we came to fight, but it is a body that is bleeding, and you lift it up and drag it through the bullets and among the screams and among the smoke and the blood. And at that moment you would risk anything to conserve what is most important, which is the passion that brought us to the Moncada, and which has its names, its look, its welcoming and strong hands, its truth in words and which can be called Abel, Renato, Boris, Mario, or any other name, but always at that moment and in the future that name is Cuba.

And there is that other moment in which neither the torture, the humiliation, nor the threats can mitigate that passion that brought us to the Moncada.

The man approached. We felt another burst of gunfire. I ran to the window. Melba ran behind me. I felt Melba's hands on my shoulders. I saw the man approach me and I heard a voice say: "They have killed your brother." I felt Melba's hands. I felt again the noise of the lead riddling my memory. I felt that I spoke without recognizing my own voice: "Was it Abel?" I looked at the man who lowered his eyes. "Is it Abel?" The man did not reply. Melba moved close to me. All of Melba was in those hands that accompanied me. "What time is it?" Melba replied: "It's nine."

These are the facts that are fixed in my memory. I don't remember anything else with precision, but from that moment on I never thought about anyone else but Fidel. We were all thinking of Fidel. We were thinking of a Fidel who couldn't die. A Fidel who had to be alive to make the revolution. The life of Fidel contained within it the life of us all. If Fidel was alive, Abel and Boris and Renato and the rest had not died, they would be alive in Fidel — who was going to make the Cuban Revolution and who was going to restore their destiny to the people of Cuba.

The rest was a cloud of blood and smoke; the rest was won by death. But Fidel would win the final battle; he would win the revolution.

Hasta la Victoria Siempre, Dear Che
Letter from Haydée to Che, after his death

Che,

Where can I write to you? You would say anywhere, to a Bolivian miner, to a Peruvian mother, to the guerrilla fighter who is or who is not but who will be. All of that I know, Che. You yourself taught me that, and moreover, this letter could not be for you. How can I tell you that I have never cried so much since the night I heard the news they killed Frank [País] — even though I didn't believe it this time. We were all sure that you were still alive, and I said: "It is not possible, a bullet cannot terminate the infinite. Fidel and you have to live, if you are not alive, how can we live?" Fourteen years ago I saw the most intensely beloved human beings die — I think that I have already lived too much. The sun is not as beautiful, I don't feel pleasure in seeing the palm trees. Sometimes, like now, in spite of enjoying life so much, knowing that it is worth opening one's eyes every morning if only for those two things, I have the desire to keep them closed, like you.

It is a fact that this continent does not deserve this. With your eyes open, Latin America would have soon found its way forward. Che, the only thing that could have consoled me is to have gone with you. But I didn't go, I am here with Fidel, I have always done what he wanted me to do.

Do you remember? You promised me in the Sierra, you said to me: "You won't miss coffee, we will drink *mate*." You were an internationalist, you had no borders, but you promised me that you would send for me when you were finally in your Argentina. And as I hoped, I knew very well that you would fulfill your promise. But it can no longer be, you couldn't, I couldn't.

Fidel said it, and so it must be true, how sad. He couldn't say "Che," he gathered up his strength and said "Ernesto Guevara," that's how he broke the news to the people, to your people. What endless sadness. I cried for the people, for Fidel, for you, because I cannot take any more. Afterwards, at your wake, this great people didn't know what rank Fidel would confer on you. He bestowed you with this: artist. I felt that all possible descriptions were too few, too small, and Fidel, as always, found the true one.

Everything you created was perfect, but you made a unique creation, you made yourself. You demonstrated that the new human being is possible, all of us could see that the new human being is a reality, because he exists, he is you.

What more can I say to you, Che? If only I knew, like you, how to say things. In any case, you once wrote me: "I see that you have become a *literati* with the power of creation, but I will confess that how I most like you is on that day in the New Year, with all of your fuses blown and firing cannons on all sides. That image, and that of the Sierra — even our fights in those days are pleasant memories — are what I will carry of you for my own use." For that reason I can never write anything of you and you will always have that memory.

Hasta la victoria siempre, dear Che,

Haydée

Published in *Casa de las Américas*, 1968

All of Us Are Part of the Same Whole

An interview with Haydée

Originally published in the magazine Santiago *in 1975, this interview was undertaken by Casa de las Americas* compañeros *in an attempt to record Haydee's valuable and illustrative memories of some of the most important events of the Cuban Revolution: the Moncada attack, the formation of the July 26 Movement, and her involvement in the urban underground. Casa republished the interview in their own magazine after Haydée's death, as a "modest attempt to contribute to the homage of the events of July 26 which will hopefully evoke the memory of the exceptional person who, to our great pride, was our leader and is our constant guide."*

How was the July 26 Movement created? How did the different existing groups — the Moncadistas, the MNR (Revolutionary National Movement), those in Oriente province — form themselves into one single organization and begin to attract new compañeros *from other political backgrounds?*

It is difficult for me to recall dates and even certain events with precision. Sometimes there are things that are all fused together for me, and I don't always know if they occurred in the Sierra Maestra, in Santiago de Cuba or at the Moncada. Certain images are confused, because everything was one and the same thing, one single struggle. For me there is only one date: July 26, and two eras: before Moncada, and after Moncada.

I have to start from the moment our *compañeros* left the Isle of Pines Prison, and even a little while before, when Melba and I left the women's prison. We always had very clear directions from Fidel: we had to know where our *compañeros* were. Some of them had managed to leave Cuba, and we had to find out what country they were in and, as far as possible, get them together in one place. I don't recall now if it was Mexico or Guatemala. We also had to locate the *compañeros* who were here and had been unable to participate in the Moncada attack for various reasons — lack of weapons, family problems, various reasons — *compañeros* who had been very traumatized by the attack and who were profoundly affected by everything that had happened. We didn't even have to go out and see how they felt. They immediately came to see us. Some of them even risked visiting us in prison, in spite of our warnings against it. In other words, Melba and I didn't have to go looking for them. They came by themselves, because they couldn't bear not having been there on that July 26, and they wanted to do something. Thus, what would later become the [July 26] Movement began to take shape. We still didn't call it the Movement. It didn't have a name. At that time they referred to us as "the Moncadistas," and Melba and I were the Moncada women. A small organization arose with the objective of undertaking various tasks. The first was the publication and distribution of *History Will Absolve Me* [the transcript of Fidel Castro's speech at the Moncada trial], which I remember as being one of the most difficult tasks. Perhaps it was one of the most agonizing, because just thinking that we might fail Fidel, who had such confidence in us, was terrible. Today it seems easy, but at that time it really was very difficult. We had virtually no resources. For me, to whom everything seems easy these days, when I recall all that, I wonder how we did it. It was one of the things that always heartened me and gave me great faith, because if we could do that, we could do anything.

The work on *History Will Absolve Me* was decisive in forming the organization that we needed. For the Santiago de Cuba *compañeros*, who were also called the Moncada group, for example, it was their first concrete task. There, various Santiago people: Frank País, Vilma Espín, María Antonia Figueroa all lent valuable aid in terms of distributing that material. And, for them *History Will Absolve Me* was a revelation, because they realized there was a [revolutionary] program, and far more than a modest program for that time. A program that proposed a whole series of objectives and around which we became mobilized.

Afterwards, we worked together for the amnesty [of the Moncada political prisoners], another task that contributed to extending and reinforcing the organization. Every time there was a meeting of those so-called politicians for an election campaign, there were always groups of compañeros who shouted out: "Amnesty! Revolution! Amnesty! Revolution!" Shouting "Revolution!" when our *compañeros* were still imprisoned was no small thing, because it had repercussions for those in prison. But we never received directions from Fidel to stop doing it, despite the fact that they suffered the consequences. Of course, we in the city could always disperse, hide ourselves — some of us were caught and others not — but they were prisoners, and when they couldn't catch those of us on the outside, the prisoners were the ones who paid the price inside. Fidel preferred us to shout "Revolution!" instead of "Amnesty."

We had also begun to have contact with comrades from Havana who belonged to the MNR (Revolutionary National Movement). There were a number of them, but those I remember most are Armando Hart and Faustino Pérez. Those comrades began to visit Melba and me spontaneously, and involved themselves in our activities from the outset. They didn't do anything without consulting us. I remember once they proposed rescuing a *compañero* who was a wounded prisoner in the hospital. They came to propose their plan to us but only "if it wouldn't prejudice the *compañeros* on the Isle of Pines." We knew that any action could prejudice our *compañeros*, but we weren't going to stop for that reason. We couldn't. And they did it. In that way we got to know many *compañeros*.

When the *compañeros* were released from the Isle of Pines, many of the finest of our youth were very inspired by and committed to Fidel and the so-called Moncadistas, because we never stopped our actions or increasing our forces. When Fidel was released, we brought him up to date with all of our contacts and told him what we thought of our *compañeros*, and I remember that he answered: "Time will tell what they will become."

When was there an agreement to form the July 26 Movement?

When Fidel came out of prison. I remember that on the ferry, during the crossing from the Isle of Pines to Batabanó — a journey that took almost the whole night — Fidel told the *compañeros* that after two or three hours with their families we were going to meet and talk. There we began to exchange ideas and Fidel proposed that we give the organization a name. He listened to each of our suggestions and I'm almost certain it was he who proposed that our group be called the July 26 Movement.

I would have liked to have called it Moncada. I had gotten used to it when people called us "Moncadistas," and we really felt great pride when Batista's henchmen scornfully labeled us "those Moncadistas...!" Melba and I were stopped on various occasions after we got out of jail, and every time they called us, "Those Moncada women!" And we felt great pride. So I was a bit attached to the idea of calling the organization Moncada. Fidel thought that calling it Moncada would limit our movement to a rather narrow framework, simply to the small group involved in the attack, and that it had to be something broader. I said that Moncada wasn't just an event, that the garrison had a significant name, but Fidel made me see that that name had been distorted, that really it was no longer the name of a great Santiago patriot.

It had become the name only of a garrison, not a patriot.

Yes. When we referred to the Moncada I didn't think of that great fighter in our War of Independence — at least until some time later — but of that blood-stained garrison. And so the name of the July 26 Movement was approved.

That was when we talked of the Movement for the first time. On many occasions, without realizing it, we had said: "No, because the Movement..." It just slipped out, then we didn't correct ourselves, and the impression remained that before the Moncada there was something called the Movement. As I recall, during the preparations for the Moncada assault, we never talked of a Movement. We talked of "the boys," of the *compañeros*. In the preceding period I had never heard even Fidel or Abel talk of the Movement. It was when Fidel and the *compañeros* left the Isle of Pines that the July 26 Movement was formed. Fidel had to leave for Mexico soon afterwards. Preparing the movement here in Cuba was truly impossible. First Raúl was in danger, then Fidel, and everything could have been lost. So the National Directorate of the July 26 Movement was formed here, as well as the Provincial Directorates, and Fidel left with a group of *compañeros* to prepare over there. He left us a precise working agenda and, moreover, continued to send us manifestos from Mexico.

In Santiago de Cuba the central task was preparing for Fidel's arrival, for the landing of the *Granma*. We knew the Oriente *compañeros* very well, especially those from Santiago: Frank and María Antonia. Vilma joined shortly afterwards. Did Vilma explain that to you?

Yes. She said that when Fidel left for Mexico she went to study in Boston and on her return stopped off in Mexico; that her initial role was to help Frank, that at that time she was "only" Frank's driver, and that it was afterwards that she had leadership responsibilities.

Vilma talked with Fidel in Mexico and when she returned she

brought a series of instructions from him for all of us, and particularly for Frank. She joined the Movement from the very beginning.
In formal terms, you could say that she did so as Frank's driver.
But being Frank's driver at that time was much more than just
that. She drove, yes, but imagine! Frank was one of the best
known and most persecuted *compañeros*. And not just anyone
could be at Frank's side. That driver knew a lot: the places, the
people, the contacts and the orders. So being his driver implied
something very special. You could say that she was his right-
hand person.

That position meant that she was a person of complete confidence?

Totally. But moreover of great courage, because there are situations in which however much a person is trusted, if they don't
also have the necessary courage, or don't know how to do what
is right at any moment... Other comrades say that they started
out as drivers. Really, that was a great responsibility, something
highly important.

When Armando and I went to Santiago in July and August
1956, Frank always insisted that Vilma drove us. Armando and
myself were also well known, and Frank feared that something
might happen to us. Everything else aside, July 26 had happened
there, and I had spent two and a half months in Boniato prison.
If I had been caught at that time in Santiago, two things would
have definitely occurred: one, I would have been imprisoned; two
— and much more seriously — my presence would have indicated
that something was going on. It would have been very difficult to
believe that I would go to Santiago if it weren't to prepare for
something there. That could have been very dangerous for the
Movement, and so it was logical that Frank feared for our safety.
If he was worried because he hadn't seen us and we assured
him that we were traveling with her: "Ah, all right! If you're with
Vilma, there's no problem."

They say that you had great skill in disguising yourself and that you could pass unnoticed in any situation.

I don't believe that it was a skill, although I did go unnoticed on most occasions. I have always had a great facility for putting on weight. Just wanting to put on a little I have gained 20 pounds as if it were nothing. And if I wanted to slim down, I could lose weight as well. That and a different hairstyle, short or long hair, made me look like a different person — so different that it was hard to recognize me. I could also be very calm and I think that that was one of the things that most helped me move around freely in Santiago. It was amazing that I could move about with such ease...

I acquired that cool head because it was highly necessary. Moncada had happened and I was concerned that being a recognized person would not allow me to participate fully. And for me that was fundamental. It was more important than my life. I needed to do things, move about, work, because if I didn't, life had no meaning. It gave me tremendous peace of mind to be able to face anything.

I remember that one night, Vilma and I were hiding out in Ruiz Bravo's house and saw the police arriving. Vilma always had a bag with her. It was a paper bag containing Frank's correspondence, and later, Daniel's papers. I told her: "Vilma, Vilma, run, take the bag!" Vilma grabbed the bag, started to run, got on to the roof and said: "Yeyé, Yeyé, run!" and I replied: "No, no, I'll come in a minute!" So, when I saw that Vilma was about to jump — I don't know how she didn't break a leg, because she jumped from a good height — I said to the people in the house: "Let me open the door." I opened the door, received the guys: "What do you want?" "We've been informed that there are people hiding in here." "Well, OK, come in... Would you like some coffee?" I gave them coffee. "Would you like a drink?" I gave them drinks. Then they began the search and I accompanied them through all the rooms: "Have a good look, have a good look so that we don't have to go through this every day." Any room or closet that they hadn't searched, I said to them: "Come on, have a look." Of course, there were some little nooks where things were hidden — documents, letters — but before they moved on in their search, I would open places for them: "Have a look here," "have a look there." I had some letters from Armando, I don't remember if he was a prisoner or in the Sierra, but I know he wasn't in Santiago. I had hidden those letters in the fold of a curtain and, of course, I never invited them to look there. Finally, they completed their search. They asked for more coffee, I served them coffee, they shook hands with me, and I still said to them: "If you need to search here again, don't worry, you can come back."

When those guys left, everyone in the house — all nine or 10 of them involved in the Movement — collapsed half fainting. On the outside, I acted as though everything was normal, but inside I was... Imagine, after all that, it was only afterwards that we realized we had received the police in our nightclothes.

Vilma returned shortly afterwards, confident that I had escaped to another place, and when they told her that I had greeted the police, had served them coffee and everything that had happened, she was... And I'm telling you that I did it with such tranquility because I had always believed that nothing would ever happen to me. Because nothing happened to me at the Moncada and everything had worked out well for me on other occasions, I felt, I don't know why, that nothing could happen to me. And that feeling grew stronger when nothing happened to me that day either.

You must remember what happened to Vilma when, jumping over the wall, those on the other side believed she was an apparition...

Ah, yes. Vilma was wearing a light-colored nightdress, very long and as she is so tall, with her long hair loose, the people on the other side were very religious and so when they saw her tumble over the wall, with such a huge jump that she virtually fell into the kitchen of the house, they even crossed themselves. They believed a virgin had appeared before them. We laughed a lot over that story, and I used to say to her: "Vilma, the Virgin of Charity or the Virgin Mary?"

You and compañero *Hart arrived in Santiago de Cuba three or four months before November 30 [1956]. What tasks were you carrying out? Why was your underground presence needed there? What were your responsibilities?*

Well, mine at least was a desire to be there. On various occasions Fidel had sent me messages saying that I should go to Mexico. He was worried that I would be taken prisoner if I stayed in Cuba. I never said "no," but I didn't go, because I had a great fear that afterwards, due to some circumstance or other, I would have to remain in Mexico. I always thought: If I am in Cuba, wherever Fidel lands I will find him, wherever it is, I will be there. But, how would I get to Cuba from Mexico? That weighed upon me so much that the first time we met up in the Sierra, I told him about it. "I would never have left you," he answered, "you would never have been left behind."

But meanwhile you were carrying out a series of missions.

Of course. Armando and I belonged to the National Directorate of the Movement, meaning that we always had duties awaiting us. In Santiago we worked very closely with Frank, but he took great care during those months that Armando and I didn't get involved in the activities of Action [urban underground], which was his front. Every time we said that we wanted to do something, he replied that it was impossible, that he understood us, but that we had to save ourselves for the decisive action (which turned out to be the attack of November 30). But of course, we weren't idle. From morning till night we were in Vilma's house, the house in San Jerónimo Street. There we discussed plans, and Armando also devoted himself to writing ideological material for the newspaper and other publications we circulated.

At that time we slept in a guest house; incredible, isn't it? Armando was known as *Jacinto*, a university professor, and I was *María, Jacinto's* wife. The only person who knew who we really were was Silvina, the owner of the guest house, and Dr. Martorell, a neighbor on the block, who had become very close to Melba and myself after we got out of prison. But there were many guests there who had no idea who we really were until much later. I even passed myself off as apolitical. In that guest house, there were frequent comments on what was going on; I remember that I said: "Well, as far as I'm concerned, as long as *Jacinto* is at the university and they don't bother him, and he can work in peace... and given the way things are, I go with him early in the morning because I wouldn't like to think of anything happening to him." We left in the early morning and returned late at night and, of course, we never went near the university. They thought that I was very jealous over *Jacinto* and made a joke out of that. We slept in that house until after November 30, for some months afterwards.

The underground front was very strong then?

Very strong. I remember that the evening before November 30, we said goodbye to Silvina and told her that we weren't going to sleep there that night. Silvina always had to know when we would arrive, because she would instantly report that we were all right. So, she asked us what was going on. I told her that she shouldn't worry, that we were simply not going to sleep there that night. Just before leaving I went to give her a hug but I didn't dare, I thought such a gesture could give her the impression that something bad was going to happen; so I took a shawl that I was wearing — a fine wool one that my brother Aldo had brought me from Mexico and which I was very attached to — and said to her: "Look, Silvina, it's a present for you, take it," and she took it, looked hard at me and without saying a word clutched it to her breast.

Armando and I always recall Silvina with great affection; for us she was a very generous person, affectionate on days when we needed that so much. I'm sure she still has that shawl, that she kept it as something especially appreciated.

Well, on the night of November 30 we turned up to sleep in Silvina's house after all. When she saw us arrive her eyes widened, but as there was so many people about, I came in saying: "Well, Silvina, we're back." She couldn't say anything. A lot had gone on in the city that day and the guests were a bit agitated. So, in a totally normal voice I said: "We went to see relatives, but imagine, we didn't dare come back, with the streets how they are in Santiago! What in the world has been going on in Santiago?"

And it was precisely in Silvina's house that Armando and I had one of the greatest experiences of that period; we were waiting for Fidel's message, the password with which he was to advise us of the *Granma* landing... I don't remember exactly, but I think there were going to be two messages. Aldo, my brother, was to receive one in Havana, I think, and Arturo Duque de Estrada the other one in Santiago. And they had to contact each other, if I remember rightly, to confirm the password... Well, Frank arrived at the house asking for us — he didn't go there very often — and entered the room almost without knocking.

Frank wasn't a very tall man, he was shorter and slimmer than Armando. I'm telling you this because he rushed in and grabbed Armando, took him in his arms and lifted him up, I don't know how. And he was saying: "*Jacinto, Jacinto*, yes *Jacinto*, yes!" "But what's going on Frank?" I asked. And he grabbed me: "*María, María*, yes *María*, yes, yes!" We didn't know what was happening.

He waved a piece of paper aloft and said: "Yes, now we can do it!" and I took the piece of paper, read the telegram with the password. The *Granma* had left.

I will never forget Frank's face. It was one of the most joyful expressions that I have ever seen. And Frank was not a joyful person. He had a profoundly sad smile, I always felt that. I know that there are times when, in someone's absence, you begin to see things differently, but I always saw him that way, those sad, sad eyes. He smiled habitually, but gave me the impression that he was sad, very sad. I believe that one of the few times that I saw Frank with a genuine smile and with happy eyes was on that day. Frank was very organized, very disciplined. He expected an unqualified military discipline even of himself. I am not referring to his relation with the Action and Sabotage [urban underground] groups — because that was logical — but Frank was very strict with his personal discipline.

Many testimonials attest to that.

I remember that when we met with Fidel in the Sierra, while we were all talking — all night was too short to tell each other everything — Frank began to check the *compañeros'* weapons, the few arms left from the *Granma*. He noticed that they were dirty and began to clean them one by one. And while we were talking, he continued listening. He was there at our side but cleaning, cleaning, cleaning... I think he even cleaned Che's weapon.

Che related that exact story in one of his most emotive passages on the revolutionary guerrilla movement. He described what Frank did as "a silent lesson."

It's because Frank was an emotional person. That was very much one of his characteristics — he always talked sparely and with precision — he spent most of the evening doing that task, and only commented: "You've gotten them a bit dirty."

That occurred on the first journey to the Sierra.

After the landing there followed a few days of expectation, because the information on the Granma *compañeros was very uncertain, right? The arrival of the first reliable news must have been exhilarating.*

Ah yes! Faustino's arrival... But the first news arrived beforehand. I remember that one day a message came that a wounded Moncada *compañero* had come down from the Sierra and wanted to see me. He insisted that it must be me. We were surprised at his insistence — why me, exactly? The message, though, was brought by someone of complete confidence and, although Frank didn't want me to go, I went to meet that *compañero*. It turned out to be Albentosa with a bullet in his neck, a terrible wound. Naturally, at first that scared me: "How had he been able to come down from the mountains? How had he managed to get here?" But then it became clear why he insisted on seeing me. He knew that if I went, because I knew him personally and the other *compañeros* didn't, that any doubts about him would be dismissed instantly.

You can imagine how thrilled I was to see Albentosa. He was the first to come to us from the Sierra. We didn't want to talk much with him, as we were worried that it would hurt him. Blood spurted from the wound when he spoke and he couldn't breathe very well. But he was able to tell us something of the combat and, most importantly, he confirmed that Fidel was alive. I couldn't leave Albentosa in that situation. His wound worried me, I urged him to get medical attention and, in addition, I felt that the house wasn't secure for him or for the family who lived there because their cover had been blown. I proposed that we get him out of there.

Albentosa is a typical Santiagüero, of mixed race, what here in Havana they call mulatto. I left with him on my arm walking through the streets of Santiago de Cuba. We dressed him in one of those turtleneck sweaters to cover his wound — he had come down from the mountains with his neck wrapped in a towel —

and set off walking as if nothing was going on.

You felt sure that nothing would happen to you and so he would be safe if he went with you?

Yes, that was it. That's it exactly. I remember that we went first to a doctor's house. From there we went to another house as the doctor instructed. And all that by foot on the sidewalks of Santiago. When he had recovered sufficiently, we made arrangements to send him to Havana. Albentosa remembers that very clearly. I heard him relating it a few months ago in a very nice way. He had expected me to be in disguise but I arrived just as I was. After we talked, I said to him: "Look, now we're going to so-and-so's house." "And how are we getting there?" he asked. "We're walking..." And he thought: "Walk about Santiago like this? She's crazy. This woman is trying to set me up..." While we were walking I was chatting to him about unimportant things, an ordinary conversation between two people walking down the street.

Well now, Faustino's arrival was something else, because it came at a very special moment.

One day, already into December [1956] — although I don't remember the date — it came out in the papers that Fidel was dead and that his family could go to see his body in Bayamo. I could never accept that Fidel was dead, not at the Moncada, or after the landing; I couldn't, just couldn't. But on that occasion, I don't know why, I admitted that it could be true, so much so that it really defeated me. I'm not easily defeated, I'm pretty optimistic. So, not wanting Armando or Frank or Vilma to see me in that state, I went to María Antonia's house. I arrived, went to the bathroom, washed my face so that she wouldn't notice my reddened eyes, but my grief was so great that however much I tried to look calm, Cayita — María Antonia's mother, quite the psychologist — noticed that something was wrong with me. She said: "What's the matter?" "Ay, Cayita, I have to tell somebody. My heart has always told me that Fidel is alive, but I feel that he is dead..."

And Cayita, very optimistic, quite euphoric — even at 70-something you should see her — told me: "Haydée, how can you say such a thing? It's not true! You'll see, in two or three days the news will arrive that Fidel is OK." She told me so many, many things that, because I had a great need to believe them, the truth cheered me and I wound up convinced that yes, Fidel was alive and we would soon receive the confirmation. And she said to me: "Stop being silly, go to Vilma's house and you'll see that in a few days the news will arrive here, because Fidel is going to imagine the concern of all of us with what the papers and the radio are saying."

We were sure that when Fidel sent someone down from the Sierra he would send that person to Cayita's house. He wrote to her address from Mexico and the *compañeros* who had been with him in Mexico knew it. And Cayita said to me: "When the message arrives, I'm going to phone you at Vilma's house and I'm going to say 'Yeyé, come and eat meringues,' and that means that the message has come." She used to make the tastiest meringues that both Armando and I adored. So it was a very natural password.

I went to Vilma's house. And every time the phone rang I ran to answer it thinking it would be her. The phone was constantly ringing there, so you can just imagine. Finally, after a few days, the phone rang. It was Cayita. But she was so excited that instead of saying what we had agreed, she repeated: "Yeyé, meringues, little meringues, super meringues! Meringues, little meringues, super meringues!" "Cayita, but...?" "Meringues, little meringues, super meringues!"

And nobody could get anything else out of her. Armando and I were saying: "What's happening?" "I don't know." And Frank said: "What's happening?" I had told them about the password, and I answered Frank: "Meringues, little meringues, super meringues," and he took the phone. "What's that Cayita?" The same thing. All of us grabbing the phone until Frank reacted: "Hey! Somebody's arrived! I'll go."

I left a little before, in a rush, with Cayita's voice echoing in my head. But instead of taking the sidewalk by Vilma's house, I went ahead on the opposite sidewalk. And I heard Frank's voice start to shout — all this in Vilma's block, which is very long — embracing and lifting up Faustino yelling, "Doctor! Doctor!" That's what we called him in the underground — all of this in the middle of the block. And I looked from one side to the other; everyone was sticking their heads out of their windows and doors... When we went into Vilma's house, I remember that Faustino himself said: "Look, this isn't the Sierra Maestra, if someone turns up now to grab us, what will happen?" But 10 minutes later the people of that San Jerónimo block began to send us little notes: "Patrol passed by. Be careful." "Army jeep seen in the neighborhood. Take care." In a word, they were concerned about us and protected us: "If you need anything, let us know." The entire block was looking after us.

Once again Santiago in solidarity...

That was tremendous. The reaction of the Santiago people was so great, so heartening, that November 30 was one of the happiest days of my life after having survived the Moncada. To experience that solidarity was something I will never forget. How many times Armando and I have recalled it! Melba and I had already felt it when we were in prison. And now, on that November 30, we began to realize that more and more families were leaving their doors open to help us hide or to help people they didn't even know escape, pulling us up on to their roof, hiding us, so we didn't fall into the hands of those killers. The low number of casualties we had on November 30 was due to the solidarity of Santiago's people.

The plan we had made with Frank was to withdraw to the Sierra to meet up with Fidel once we had completed the actions in support of the landing in Santiago. We gave ourselves the task of preparing a truck with weapons and food — in that house there was an impressive quantity of eggs and we boiled them all. We all got into the truck. A contingent of *compañeros* was to go with us in that vehicle. There had already been fierce fighting at various points in the city. We debated whether leaving for the Sierra would be possible, as the army must be cracking down. We sent a jeep ahead to see if the roads were blocked. The exit route was already impossible; the highways were blocked by dictatorship troops. All we could do was to fight and then scatter within the city itself.

In the beginning there was a large number of combatants in the house, but when we saw that helicopters were flying overhead, missions were given to the *compañeros* so that they would distance themselves from the place without getting caught, first the women and then the men, finally leaving a much smaller group. We presumed that the house must have been discovered already, given certain accounts brought by *compañeros* who came to report that they had completed their actions. Frank wanted to stay fighting there to the end, to give Fidel and his *compañeros* more time to land and get up into the hills.

That day, I relived with tremendous vividness our experience during the assault on the Moncada, when we were left waiting there while they surrounded us, and we couldn't get out. I had always thought that if we had left a bit earlier, many comrades would have survived, maybe even Abel. We also knew many people in Santiago had reached out to the *compañeros* who had participated in the Moncada assault, and thanks to their help, some of them had been able to escape. Because of this, I continued to believe that things could have been different.

And so on November 30, when Frank proposed that we should go on fighting until the end in the house on Santa Lucía and San Félix, the memory of what happened assailed me once again. In the case of the Moncada it had been necessary to keep on fighting to guarantee's Fidel's retreat to the hills. Obviously, if they had immediately surrounded us in Santa Lucía there would have been no other remedy than to fight, but I could still see excellent possibilities of getting out, and moreover I realized that the park we were occupying wasn't suitable for any sustained action. In those circumstances it was preferable to fight in the streets and die on the streets if that was the only alternative.

History was once again repeating itself, in another way. The facts came together again in another form and intermingled: there was an Abel again, there was a Boris, there was a Melba. Once again much loved people at my side. No, [Moncada] could not be repeated. We had to get out into the street, fire on the killers, seek them out rather than wait for them. It was a thousand times preferable to die like that than to be alive and surrounded once again. On the other hand, I was certain that some people could be saved.

Due to my insistence, Frank finally made the decision to leave the house. He was in charge of the action but I sensed the need to appeal to him as a Moncada combatant to make him listen to my point of view. And I told him, moreover, that he had a duty to live, that he had to stay alive because Fidel needed him. He finally accepted my proposal, so we dispersed. Frank headed for the school where the *compañeros* were still fighting, to see what had become of a mortar that we had there, and exchanged shots with the guards. We didn't discover that until afterwards, because it was two days before he appeared at Vilma's house. Armando and I left with Vilma shortly afterwards for the San Jerónimo house.

Many *compañeros* were saved thanks to those doors left open by Santiago families. There were so many times on other occasions when Armando and I were returning from a mission, or there was a burst of gunfire, or we saw a patrol approaching, that we would go into the first house we saw and say: "How are you," and ask for a glass of water. They would give us coffee, and when the patrol had gone by: "Well, see you later, thanks." Nobody asked any questions. And I am not talking about people who knew us, because we ducked into the nearest doorway we could find. Of course, if a patrol had surprised us and attacked in the street, we would have had to stand our ground. We weren't going to run inside a house to fight from there, risking the lives of an entire family.

When was the departure for the Sierra decided?

After Faustino came down. I don't exactly recall how we worked it out. We left for Manzanillo. There we met up with Celia and Guerrita Matos, and there we met Herbert Matthews, the U.S. journalist for the *New York Times*. We reached a certain point, got out and began to walk in separate groups. Matthews went first and then us, but we didn't have to walk far because Fidel and the *compañeros* agreed on a nearby venue for the meeting. Certain things were done to give this first journalist the impression that we had controlled a large territory and had a large army. But in truth, there were only a few people there with Fidel — 12 or 15 comrades, with very few weapons, almost barefoot, with pitiful clothing. They had to give the most presentable clothes and boots to the *compañeros* who got close to Matthews and then trade clothes again when a new *compañero* passed by him, so that Matthews wouldn't see the real situation.

I also recall that some shots were heard during that visit and Fidel, who knew they weren't ours — though they all sounded the same to me — said: "That's Batista's army. They don't dare come up here. They know that we are strong here and they don't dare, those cowards don't dare to ascend." I was so happy to hear that! In that first journey to the Sierra, Frank and I were talking on the way of the need to get Fidel out of the Sierra, of finding a way of getting the *compañeros* out of there, to reorganize them elsewhere, to start a new push that would offer a better guarantee of success. Frank sincerely believed that it was too risky for Fidel, that the survival conditions at that time in the Sierra were very difficult. I agreed with Frank. "Well, are you going to tell him?" "Yes, at the first opportunity we have." "Then you start the conversation and I'll support you." We went with that idea in our heads.

But then Fidel sat down to talk with us and began to ask us about everything that had happened. After we had given him all the information necessary, he turned to communicate directly with Frank and began to tell him that he needed so many bullets of such and such a kind, so many guns; asked how many had been saved from the November 30 urban uprising and when and how they were going to be sent to the Sierra. He was speaking with tremendous optimism, with great security. The only thing he needed was arms for 100 men up there; the rest was in place. And then — looking at me quite fixedly — he said that if only this much had been achieved with the Moncada, which is what he had wanted at the time. Now that they were going to collect weapons little by little, and with them we were going to attack small garrisons, collecting the weapons taken from them to further fortify and expand the group of combatants... Well, he radiated such confidence that we not only didn't propose what we had agreed but we never even remembered it. And how right he was! Can you imagine the huge mistake of leaving the Sierra, coming back in another *Granma* and going through another Alegría del Pío? That was the extraordinary thing about him — his clarity of vision.

What struck me was how safe you felt up there. That night we slept on a ledge. There was only one blanket and we slept all huddled up together to take advantage of that cover — of course those at the ends came off worst — but with all of that, I slept so deeply, even though I was underneath a bush and water was dripping on me all night. The Sierra gives you that security. Daily life there was difficult, it was very hard, particularly at the beginning: the lack of food, shelter and shoes, sleeping on the ground without hammocks, having to carry everything on foot. In the early days, moreover, everything bothered you. You hadn't grown used to it yet. But, I'm telling you, however hard that was, you felt a security. At least for me, I was up in the Sierra; I was there for a while and came down totally recovered. Of course, living underground in the city had its particular problems: you lived in constant tension, you knew they could detain you at any moment, that they could kill you at any moment. You always had to sleep with your eyes open.

After that first journey then, preparations went ahead for reinforcements?

Yes, immediately. Groups were coordinated and sent via Celia and Guerrita Matos. They were on the outskirts of Manzanillo, in an overgrown area on one side of a hut belonging to trusted *campesinos*. Bare, flat land, but terrain which allowed the men to pass quickly, because it was relatively close to where Fidel and the rest of the *compañeros* were. So as not to arouse suspicion, the men arrived there first, without utilizing jeeps or any other transportation, rested, and were then directed to the agreed location. Weapons were sent little by little by the same route, as well as other things.

Frank was arrested at that time, wasn't he?

Frank was taken prisoner, subjected to trial, and some of the *Granma* combatants who were captured were also awaiting trial.

Who replaced Frank to direct the reinforcement action?

I don't remember. At that time everybody knew what he or she had to do. The mission was clear to everybody. It was known where the weapons were, who had to go and get them, how they were going to be moved. Everything was carefully planned.

What I do remember is that Armando talked to the new *compañeros* about discipline, what Frank was entrusting them with, what Fidel expected of them. That in that moment Frank couldn't be there, but that they couldn't fail him. I don't remember who headed the action front at that time.

Returning to the reinforcements: we devoted ourselves to rescuing all the weapons that were left from the November 30 action and taking them to the safe houses. Vilma and I participated in that. Vilma as the driver, taking most of the weapons from one place to another in her car. The weapons were kept in boxes — I remember we often used refrigerator boxes. Afterwards they were dispatched in trucks. Not the bullets and other smaller items, so as not to overuse the truck journeys and blow our cover. We took the lighter items with the help of other women *compañeros*, traveling in cars. Sometimes we slept in the hut until Celia arrived, we handed over the things to her and returned home.

Did you remain in Santiago the whole time?

We made short trips to Havana, to Las Villas, but most of the time we were in Santiago. I went back to the Sierra on various occasions, until after the events of the April [1958] strike. After the second trip to the Sierra we couldn't go on using Silvina's house. That time Celia and I stayed in the Sierra for a number of weeks, and some U.S. journalists took that photo of us wearing cartridge belts. That photo was published in *Bohemia* magazine when press censorship was lifted — a copy they took from *Life* magazine. Imagine the commotion in Silvina's house: "But that's *María*!" It must have been tremendous. Silvina, feigning the same surprise, said: "*María* deceived us!" Nevertheless the people in the guesthouse showed solidarity in their attitude. They calmed Silvina down and told her that nobody there knew that *María* had been a resident at the guesthouse and nobody was going to know. And matters went no further. Silvina had no problems and even continued with the guesthouse until 1959. Moreover, she continued to take in many comrades, with the cooperation of the other residents.

[Armando] Hart was arrested on various occasions, wasn't he?

Yes. One of the times they took Armando we were together. We were in La Virgen del Camino waiting for the bus to return to Santiago from Havana. Martínez Páez was with us. He had taken us there, because it was safer to leave from that point than from the bus terminal. The three of us were waiting. It was almost dark. While they were talking I was pacing back and forth. And I was alert, watching. Then I heard various cars approaching at tremendous speed. The place was full of women and children... but there was no doubt what was happening, and I yelled out: "Armando, the cops!" and started running. Then I heard a voice behind me: "There goes Yeyé!" But I kept on running, turned a corner, ran the whole block, reached another street and realized that there were a number of cars parked there. So I got between two of those cars and squatted down. From there I sensed them following, some on foot and others in a car, passing by me on both sides. But there I stayed, quiet as a mouse, crouched down as far as I could, and I gave them the slip, they couldn't catch me. But they did get Armando and Martínez Páez. You see? They were taken prisoner and I got away...

How did you manage to get out of there?

Well, after spending a while crouched down between the two cars, I peeped out and saw a driver. I came out and said: "Listen, please help me. I had to get down there because I'm pregnant, only two months, but I think I'm going to lose it," and he immediately agreed. "Look, I'm a member of La Quinta de Dependientes (a mutual benefit society clinic), could you take me there?" That didn't just come into my head. All my family were members of La Quinta, and I knew the place well. We got there and the man was still saying to me in a very friendly way: "Do you want me to wait for you?" I told him it wasn't necessary, that they would attend to me there and advise my family, that he could go without any problem. As soon as he pulled away, I ran to one of the public telephones there and dialed like crazy, first to Armando's house. His mother Marina answered and I told her: "The SIM people [secret police] have just taken Armando" — because just as they knew me as Yeyé, we could also identify them and knew which ones were from the SIM, the Bureau, the Ventura people. I stressed: "Tell Hart (Armando's father) to go there with all the Supreme Court people, because they'll kill him if you don't act quickly. He should go to the SIM, and if they deny that they have him there, tell them that I myself saw them arrest him. They know that I was there and that I escaped." I said all this because my father-in-law was a judge in the Supreme Court, and because if he didn't intervene immediately and declare that his son was arrested, they would torture and rapidly kill him. If we acted fast, we could achieve a more "normal" trial and imprisonment.

As soon as I hung up, I called Martínez Páez's house. He had organized a reception in his house for two journalists due to arrive from the United States that same night. Marcelo Fernández was to meet them at the airport and take them to the house. Well, I dialed the number and asked for his sister. I told her: "Listen, they've just arrested Martínez Páez. Forget about that meal you've prepared and call this number." I told her to call Marcelo and tell him not to take the invited guests there but to Luis Buch's house. "But, who's calling?" "Look, don't worry about that, it's a friend who was there when he was detained, I managed to escape but he had time to ask me to give you this message." And I urged her: "Listen, if a Cuban arrives at your house with two foreigners, tell them the reception isn't there."

From La Quinta de Dependientes I left for Luis Buch's house, and luckily, everything worked out OK. We were able to locate Marcelo at the airport and give him the message. Really, everything was organized so that Armando and I would leave for Santiago, and then go on to Bayamo to wait for the journalists and go up to the Sierra with them. But given what happened, we had to change the plan. Marcelo and I agreed to set out for Manzanillo with the journalists as soon as possible. Moreover, I had another mission to fulfill at the same time: to take 5,000 pesos (the first time we had managed to collect a sum like that), in one-, five-, and 10-peso notes, because taking 100-peso bills to the Sierra made no sense — who was going to change them up there? So, I wrapped the bundle up in a plastic bag and stuck it to my body with tape, so as to appear pregnant — this idea occurred to me because of the story I'd given the driver who got me out of La Virgen del Camino. And, so we were able to leave for Manzanillo the following day, Marcelo and I with the two journalists. We got to Manzanillo but, of course, nobody was waiting for us there. Armando's arrest had already been announced on the radio. We had to circle around and around, with the journalists asking Marcelo if something was going on — he was the only one who spoke English. And Marcelo made them believe that the circling about was the password. Finally I remembered a safe contact of ours in Manzanillo; we went there and everything was worked out.

Was that the time that Hart escaped during the trial?

Yes. That was another thing... Armando knew the place very well, because he had acted as state attorney there on various occasions. When the trial started I was in Havana on some mission. He managed to get a message to me asking me to send him a T-shirt "because the prison uniform was irritating his skin," and he stressed that it must be a T-shirt and not a shirt. I got the T-shirt to him without ever suspecting what was behind that request. He didn't get in contact with the Movement, but acted "off his own bat," because he thought that the Movement would counsel against it. Fortunately he was able to pull it off safely.

Armando was not being tried alone. There were other detainees in various circumstances. They took them to court in a group, something that they did on various occasions. They never entered by the front door of the Palace of Justice. They drove them there in prison wagons. They took them up to the court by the back entrance, the courtroom was on the top floor. He remembered that on the second floor, close to the stairway, there was a little door; he also realized that each time they took them to court there was one guard for 15 prisoners. The day he escaped, he had managed to place himself in the middle of one of those groups of 15 and had the cooperation of the *compañero* behind him. When they were close to the little door, that person said in a low voice: "Armando, Armando." Armando managed to reach the little door. On the way down the stairway he took off his prison jacket — he had the T-shirt on underneath — and with that T-shirt and the prison pants, he had quite a disguise. He left by the main entrance to the Palace of Justice, while the guards were watching the back entrance. How ridiculous for the dictatorship people! Nobody even noticed his absence until they called for him in the courtroom: "Armando Hart Dávalos," and he failed to appear.

Even his father, who was in the courtroom, created a terrific fuss because he thought that they had done something to his son, until he was told: "Don't worry, Armando has escaped." When the news came out on the radio, which was how I heard about it, I couldn't believe it, and after Armando's escape we returned to Santiago on Frank's orders. And we continued with the underground struggle.

Armando was to fall prisoner again, a year after that. They caught him coming down from the Sierra, before the April [1958] strike.

I went through that year in constant fear for Armando. I knew that the danger for him was greater than ever, that his flight was going to provoke increased persecution. We went up and down the Sierra various times. The time they caught him, I hadn't gone... as seemed to be the way of things.

That must have been a very difficult year?

I can tell you, that was a year in which I was obsessed with Armando's security, watching out night after night. I was only calm when he was in the Sierra.

It's amazing that you visited him in prison.

That was after the April [1958] strike. When the strike began I was in the Sierra. Afterwards it was agreed that I should leave the country. When I came down to Santiago, I was told that Armando was feeling very bad. During that time they had killed his brother Enrique and the strike had failed. It was Ramona Ruiz Bravo who almost always went to visit him and moreover she told me that he was going to escape, but they were watching him very closely on account of his previous jail break. He was in Boniato jail, where I had been imprisoned after Moncada. So I decided to go and see him, without saying anything to Daniel, because he would obviously forbid it, given that I could be recognized there. I said that I was Armando's sister, Martha Hart, and the chief there authorized me to go. So I went. And when Armando saw me, my God, what a tremendous surprise! So I told him why I had come, that they had told me how he was feeling, and that it couldn't be, he wasn't to do anything stupid. And I told him that I was going abroad. Nobody recognized me in the prison. You see how nothing ever happened to me? But I recognized them; I saw some faces there, faces that made my flesh crawl!

He remained in prison for the rest of the war?
Yes. He was on the Isle of Pines. He got out on January 1, 1959.

You continued going up into the Sierra until April 1958, right?
While he was in prison I went up there a lot. I wasn't "blown," although that might be hard to believe, because, well, Celia reached a point when she couldn't go down, she had to stay up there because her cover had been blown. But I was going up and coming down, I continued to fulfill various missions, including during the April strike.

I remember that because of the strike there weren't enough weapons in the Sierra for an assault on Batista's troops. We had mines with which to halt enemy tanks and vehicles, and ambush columns, but there weren't enough detonators for those mines. I talked with Fidel, I asked him to let me go down, assured him that I could get the detonators and return, and return in time. Fidel absolutely refused. But I insisted and insisted: "They won't get me, I'm sure they won't get me." And, in the end, I got his authorization.

Everything went well in Santiago and for the return I reverted to using the "pregnancy" ploy to hide the detonators. I did it so well that I not only looked like a pregnant woman, but if I was touched, I felt like one as well. I went back quickly in a car used to making that journey. When I arrived at Bueycito, they stopped the car. Luckily the car had no problems and I carried everything off, with my pregnancy smock and *campesina* look. I created a real scene there: "What's going on? But what's going on? Look, I went to Bayamo to see the doctor because I was feeling bad, and I can't take any shocks. I'm going to the sawmill. If there's any problem let the soldiers come with us please. I'm trusting in you to get there, because I don't want to think of the insurgents coming out on the way." And everything worked out so well that they gave us a soldier to escort us to the sawmill, which spared us more stops, checks and explanations. We reached the sawmill and I told the soldier not to worry, that he could go back because from there I only had to walk a little stretch to find the mule that would take me to my house. And they left me there. That Bueycito business was really something for me. Just thinking about what I was carrying! Can you imagine?

When was it decided that you should leave the country?

After the failure of the April strike there was a big meeting with the people from the Sierra (Che, the *compañeros* and us). It was then that Fidel proposed the idea to me. I never thought that was going to happen. I was always afraid to leave Cuba. So much so that I didn't want to go to Mexico. I always felt a great need to be here in my homeland, whatever the circumstances. And Fidel knew that. At that time it was difficult for Fidel to talk to me, so difficult that I readily accepted his proposal. In reality, I wouldn't have accepted it from anybody else. He told me he was going to ask me something very difficult, that he had chosen me because I knew the grave conditions in the Sierra, that I had to go. I said to him: "All right, Fidel, if there's no alternative..." He said: "Good, I knew you'd do it, I have confidence in you, I wanted you to do it."

I went to Miami. The only thing that I asked was that he let me choose my own way and that he shouldn't worry, that they weren't going to grab me. I didn't want to enter an embassy, or leave as an exile. I had the feeling that would make it harder for me to return to Cuba at any given moment. I left for Camagüey, went down to Santiago, talked with Daniel — who was already heading Action [the urban underground] — and traveled with

Marcia, Lester Rodríguez's wife, a young woman with tremendous authority, with whom I had already undertaken two or three missions. I reached the airport early, and she came later. If something happened to me, she wouldn't take the flight and would report what had happened; if not, she would board normally after me, and we would continue on together. There, people supported us, too. When I arrived and handed over my fake passport, which bore another name and another photo, the guy looked at me, looked at the name, the photo, looked at me, and said: "Wait there."

I approached Marcia furtively and said: "Look, I think they've found me out, so go to the end of the line, so that if something happens to me you can leave." I was unsure whether to proceed or not. But when the line was already moving on one side, the guy reappeared: "Come this way please." I protested: "Yes, yes, but people are already boarding..." And he replied: "Yes, but there wasn't a place for you and we've found one." He took me by the arm, took me somewhere else and put me on to the plane bypassing the other controls. Marcia, who saw that move but didn't hear what he said to me, ran after us and challenging the guy: "Hey, they told me I couldn't go and since she's after me that means I get to go too!" She got tough: "So, there weren't any seats, right? That's a lie, there were loads..." But the guy said to her: "See if you can board too, go on." And she was still saying to him: "Tell them!" Then, when I was about to go up the boarding steps to the plane, he gave me his hand, looked a bit embarrassed, and said to me: "Good luck!"

Fifteen years later, not long ago, I met him in Camagüey and he greeted me and said: "Hey, Haydée Santamaría, you don't remember me, do you?" I stood there looking at him, because I might forget names but I remember faces very well. "Something comes to mind, something a long time ago, are you from my town? Are you from Encrucijada?" He reminded me of someone from my youth... "I was the guy who shook your hand when you were taking the plane for Miami. Do you think you deceived me?" "Of course not," I answered, "you wished us good luck and everything!" Then he told me that in the airport the employees "squeezed" passengers to get the money for the tickets, and that he had used the pretext that he was going to "squeeze" me because that was a much surer way of leaving, because you didn't have to go through passport control.

When you arrived in the United States was there an existing organization of the movement?

It was very divided, with many problems, as in all those places where there is no direct combat. The movement was broken into the various organizations and there were many problems, but something had already been done. We devoted ourselves to organizing all those people and sending things to Cuba. Many *compañeros* there were dying to do something, and so it was extremely difficult for them. I believe it was seven months I spent out of Cuba and I have never talked about it before because it was such a painful part of my life. There are other incidents that were very painful; but I recall them with emotion and love, even the most painful ones. But that period was such a bitter one that I have never spoken of it before. I had never been there and it was terrible getting to know that country. I had to get mixed up with people of the worst kind, with the Mafia...

Acquiring arms was done in contact with gangsters?

Of course, among those people and other people like that to get the money. I think that was the most stressful part, the sacrifice was so great. It's a horrible country! Well, being here in Cuba was my raison d'être. Although there were dangers, it was different.

That was in 1958?

I must have arrived at the end of April or the beginning of May. Our mission was to raise funds among the Cubans and to obtain arms. But the extremely limited number of arms that reached our *compañeros* here didn't come from the United States. It's a fact that no boat or plane was allowed to leave from the United States. There were other, easier places we could send weapons from, but in terms of the United States it was just the small arms that our *compañeras* could conceal in their skirts, at great risk and without solving the main problem of the Sierra, which was that of long-range weapons. We risked such fine women *compañeras* to bring in a few little pistols that could only be used for self-defense in the city. The need was great and there was no alternative, but it all fell far short of what was really needed.

We did purchase arms for the Sierra, we spent thousands and thousands of pesos, more than one million, but they never reached the Sierra. We bought a plane that cost $25,000 and then it never left Miami, because the authorities blocked it. We bought a small boat and it never left Miami. We bought those little pleasure boats that were in fashion there, which many people had. And not one of those boats ever left.

That's why I can't understand how boats can leave and attack our fishermen now. Where do they come from, who protects them? We could never do it even with the smallest craft, and now fantastic speedboats are coming out. I'm telling you that you need tremendous backing for that. They would always catch us before we left. And there was no snitch among the Cubans there.

And now look at the ease they have with those good speedboats! They leave, enter, shoot at our fishermen, kill our fishermen, and "the culprits are unknown!" We did it clandestinely, with Cubans that were good people, organized to undertake revolutionary tasks, and they got [the boats] for us, but we couldn't leave.

Some of the armaments that arrived came from other places, like Venezuela when Larrazábal was there, but never from the United States. Sometimes we managed to get a light aircraft through, with bits and pieces, but good armaments, no. More than $1 million were spent, money laboriously and even painfully collected, and only those few little bits reached Cuba. We could only get something through when we had made a small purchase and then committed ourselves to another huge purchase. They wouldn't denounce the first, in order to grab the big business that followed. But imagine at what price we got hold of the few weapons from the first bid. They let that rubbish pass to grab the next. And meanwhile we'd send the bullets. But I'm telling you that the few bullets that arrived here must have ended up costing about $25 each.

But planes! Once a plane cost us $50,000. Naturally, we fell prey to inexperience, desperation, because later I didn't agree with trying to send the stuff; later, everything stayed there. It was better to help the *compañeros* in places where it was more feasible to send arms with that money.

However, the Yankees perpetuated the myth that the revolution had received indirect aid from the United States by betraying its "good faith." Well, if that war had been fought only with arms that came from the United States, we would all have been dead.

Look, those seven months were so terrible for me, so terrible, that when I came back [to Cuba] on January 2, one of those guys, from the CIA or wherever, came to see me in order "to close my case" — because they arrested me some five months after arriving [in the United States] and I had to present myself to the police every Saturday — he came to see me to say "please, would I clarify how I had entered their territory."

Didn't you enter the United States legally?
Well, I entered "legally" but with a false passport. It wasn't in my

name. Five months later they arrested me, but without knowing who I was. One of those guys we bought weapons from must have informed on me — although I tried to avoid showing my face to those people, at some point it must have been that, don't you think? So, the passport they took from me had another name, and this guy arrived to ask how I got into the country, that he needed that information in order "to close the case." And I said to them: "That's what you're here for, so you find out. I have read in all the books that you have the most experienced secret service in the world, so you find out. If I have to tell you how a poor, unfortunate woman like me entered your country; well, you charge enough money for that, you find out, that's what they pay you for."

And still he persisted: "If you don't say how you entered you're never going to be able to come to this country again." Trying to say they could keep me from returning! "Look, I will enter this country with a diplomatic passport, and if you don't let me enter with a diplomatic passport, I've still got the route from last time. So, if I tell you where, I'll make things difficult for myself. "See you later."

I still don't know if they have closed the case yet.

How did you feel arriving back in Cuba again?

Imagine! I was happy, I was sad. Happy to find myself free, walking through the streets of my country without them following me, without fear. But also expecting so many things that I didn't see. Happy at the triumph and for everything we hoped to do, but pained at the absence of beloved faces. That made us feel terrible in those days: faces that we knew were no longer but that we also expected to see and that we missed. Then finding the Sierra comrades exhausted, like I found Camilo Cienfuegos. I went to Ciudad Libertad [previously Batista's military headquarters] and when he saw me he didn't even recognize me. I found him worn out, completely worn out, stretched out on a bed and I sat down beside him and took his hand: "Camilo." "And who are you?" "But Camilo, you really don't know me?" He had spent two weeks without sleeping. And I arrived so well rested, fresh, without having lost one night of sleep! It was very painful for me not to have been in Cuba with them at that time, it really was... And so I called for a doctor to see him, and he gave him something, because by then he couldn't sleep, and he refused to take anything in order to sleep: "There's so much left to do, Yeyé, so much..." It's selfish, I've been in many actions, and it seems like you want everything for yourself, but really and truly, I dreamed of the hardest times in the Sierra, suffering for not having been there with them.

I'm asthmatic, I had some very hard times in the Sierra and when I felt most tired, I managed to go on by thinking of the day we would go down and find ourselves in Santiago de Cuba. I didn't see that. I really dreamed that. I would say to myself: "Ay, well, now I'm climbing the rocky ledges, I'm just about finished," and I almost couldn't, but the column never had to wait for me, it was difficult for everyone, but I comforted myself by thinking: "One day we'll go down, one day we'll enter Santiago de Cuba by this same route."

And truthfully I would have stayed there all my life. I would either have entered Santiago with the rebels or remained fighting in Santiago with the militia, which is the same thing, isn't it? Being there with my comrades.

I arrived on January 2, first of all because I wanted to take out all the Cubana airplanes that had remained in the United States, so they couldn't try to impound them. The pilots had deserted and so I sought out pilots in the United States. I fixed it so that all those planes returned here, they had to be here. I presented myself as an official delegate of the Cuban Revolution, of Fidel, and I was able to get them all out. I arrived on January 2, and saw Camilo so skinny that he couldn't even open his eyes, exhausted, exhausted and me so fresh, so rested...

But you had fulfilled an extremely important role there.

Well, I did what could be done. But what I wanted was to come back. Fidel had told me that as soon as I had collected $1 million I could return, and I exceeded that figure. I was counting on returning but it seemed unjust at that moment to say: "I'm coming next month," with the problems they had here.

Would you say something now about Frank? About Frank and Daniel. Frank was very young, right? Young but with great maturity. Is that how you remember Frank? Was that always a trait of his or was it accentuated with the responsibilities of the struggle?

One of the things I remember from the first time I met Frank is his youthful face. What amazed me wasn't Frank maturing in the struggle, but his maturity from the first moment I met him. He surprised me when he told me his age, he was effectively still a boy, he barely had any facial hair. The first time I met him he seemed to be a young man of few words, and then I was worried that he might have felt inhibited with me, given that I was already a woman — he was just a boy in comparison to me. And I commented on that to Armando. But Armando replied: "No, he's the same way with me." Then I began to see that Frank was very observant, something quite rare. Only a few times did I see him act like others of his age, happy or talking of parties, and I don't know why, because we had a lot of fun together.

I always remember that life in Vilma's house, in San Jerónimo Street, comparable only to life at Callé 25 and O in Havana [Abel and Haydée's apartment], which in spite of so much commitment was a youthful and happy household. In San Jerónimo I relived that same spirit, that same fraternity, and the *compañeros* happy like they were back then. But not Frank, Frank let other people do the laughing.

After knowing Frank, you became aware of his infinite sensibility, an enormous sensibility and a love for human beings, which he hid on many occasions, hid what he was feeling. I believe that in all that time that we lived in that close-knit group, Frank revealed himself as one of the most sensitive people in the face of everything that we experienced, while also showing himself to be exceptionally energetic.

All of the compañeros *were perplexed at the combination of sweetness and severity in Frank. In what way could he be so pleasant and so severe at the same time?*

It's true. There were many times in those early days in Santiago, when we had arguments about different issues — particularly ideological questions — I would recall the *compañeros* who had previously fallen in the Moncada and he, being so sensitive, without me having uttered a word, would say to me: "Haydée, don't consult so much with the dead, these are different times." And he said to me many times: "You don't think about anything other than the dead," in the best sense, to give me a lesson. After he was assassinated I received a very moving letter he had written shortly after his brother Josué's death in action, in which he asked my forgiveness for having reproached me for consulting so much with the dead, for having been so hard on me, and that now I was going to have to give him the same advice because he felt that he would be consulting Josué about everything. He said: "My little sister, I know that you will understand me, because you have always regarded me with so much affection, but now I'm going to have to consult with Josué." At the same time, I received another letter from him, dated five or six days later, in which he told me that things were getting harder by the day in Santiago. He saw his situation as being very difficult, and that he only was asking life for one more month. He told me that we should go there, that he believed however bad things were in Santiago there was less danger than in Havana. I could tell that he had overcome the most difficult moment of Josué's death. I don't know if he had time to get over it, because everything happened very quickly. He was killed only one month after his brother.

Anything one could say about Frank seems inadequate. His deeds speak louder than any words. What I can say is that we have had the opportunity to know great *compañeros* whom we will always mourn, but I can tell you that Frank is one of those that we most felt for, most cried over. Moreover, he was a real key for us. He was a part of the Sierra in Santiago, and his loss was the loss of that part of the Sierra. His death could have made the situation of our *compañeros* in the Sierra difficult, which was our greatest concern. Frank always gave tremendous priority to the Sierra *compañeros*, so his death was a great blow to us. For all of us his death was like an earthquake. Choosing who was going to replace him, who always put the Sierra before everything, was tremendously difficult. In the urban underground everything was very heroic, very brave, but it wasn't a military life like in the Sierra, you couldn't work collectively like in the Sierra. In the urban underground we were dotted here and there. You could undertake acts of exceptional valor, but they were always more or less individual actions, due to their very nature. In the Sierra, as the troops lived and acted together, actions were of a distinct collective nature, and that was the base of a new army. We understood that difference, and that had always greatly concerned Frank.

When we began to evaluate compañeros to replace Frank, many names were discussed. Well, we were in agreement — at least those of us who were close to him: Vilma, Armando and I, were totally agreed on choosing Daniel. It was very difficult to replace Frank. When we told him, Daniel was a bit shocked. He was an extremely modest man, one of those *compañeros* who always thought about who they had replaced. Many times we had to tell him that he would burn himself out thinking like that, that he had a task ahead of him and couldn't be thinking like that. But Daniel was a person of a valor and modesty that we had seen in only a few *compañeros*. We consulted with the people in the Sierra, and soon afterwards they also approved of this choice.

It's difficult to talk of fallen comrades, especially when they were so well loved. I try to be as objective as possible and I should like to be able to say everything that I feel. We saw Daniel working better day by day, making an effort to carry the burden of being the replacement for somebody as respected, beloved and outstanding as Frank, both in the Sierra and in the urban underground. Those of us who lived alongside Daniel wished that we had known more of his history.

He fulfilled his role perfectly. I never regretted having taken part in his selection. And because of my inevitable tendency to "consult the dead," one tends to make comparisons. Faced with any situation, Daniel thought about what Frank would have thought; what Frank would have done. Naturally, there were *compañeros* who thought that someone with the prestige of having arrived with the *Granma*, having been an outstanding leader in the Sierra, was a requisite for occupying that position. But we never doubted the decision. There were other very valiant *compañeros*, but we never had any doubts.

Daniel was never unworthy of the confidence bestowed on him. I saw him operating at very decisive moments for the Movement, in very conflictive circumstances, and with very hard decisions to make. I always saw him act with firmness, consciously, consulting, discussing, with a great spirit of collective leadership. He later decided to go to the Sierra and asked permission. At that time I wasn't in Cuba. I was very happy because I thought that his life would become much safer, given that his life in Santiago was already very difficult, as it was for the Movement in general. And when Vilma sent me word that Daniel was going up to the Sierra, I felt calmer and frankly, at that point I wasn't thinking about who could take his place. From that distance, I was thinking about the need to preserve Daniel's life. Daniel fell in combat, exactly one year after Frank, on the same day.

His courage and modesty were also reflected in the Sierra and at his death. Being a comrade who had not been long in the Sierra, where it took time to adapt, from the very beginning he demonstrated his capacity as a leader and as a comrade. Perhaps he didn't have all the training that a person in his position should have had, but what he did have was that stature of modesty and courage that I have seen in few *compañeros*.

We have said on many occasions that the stature of our *compañeros* is so great that sometimes one is eclipsed by the other. In this case one and the other are the same. Frank's stature was tremendous and hard to replace. But I believe that Frank and Daniel, and Daniel and Frank were so interlinked that I am sure that Frank himself would have chosen Daniel, who was one of the comrades he most respected. All of us see them as united, in our sentiments and in our thoughts. Those two figures are joined to be one. That is how we must remember them, because all of us are part of the same whole.

Casa is Our America,
Our Culture, Our Revolution

Haydée Santamaría speaks to Jaime Sarusky

This interview with well-known Cuban journalist and author Jaime Sarusky was republished in 1988 in the magazine Casa de las Américas. *Here, Haydée speaks candidly about the creation of Casa, both its troubles and triumphs over the years, and her vision of Casa's larger role as a bridge linking Cuba and the rest of Latin America.*

At 11:30 on an unusually gray and cold Havana morning, we met with Haydée Santamaría on the first floor of the Casa de las Américas. For someone unfamiliar with her unique personality it might appear strange and even surprising that it was she who asked where we would feel most comfortable for the interview and even cooperated in installing a cable for the tape recorder. Then recalling the thread of the question, she said:

There was an institution here called the Panamerican Colombista Society that supposedly had something to do with writers. When we arrived in 1959, we realized it was a fraud. It would ask for budgets for this and that, collecting money from here and there. The Ministry of Education took over the institution. I worked with Armando [Hart] in the ministry and he proposed that I should come here. So I designated certain people to find out what was here and to propose what could be done. We thought of creating an institution that would be both Cuban and Latin American. I stayed here for three months when they proposed that I direct the new institution.

You referred to that theme — cultural internationalism — a little while back when you were explaining the battle waged from the Casa de las Américas for a reconciliation of the continent's cultures.

Precisely. We saw that it was necessary to create a vehicle to attain that communication, to create a Latin American magazine. That task was not an easy one. The early editions came out until 1964. We were thinking of a serious magazine, which could be political while retaining a cultural aspect. We didn't have anyone to appoint as editor and then [Roberto Fernández] Retamar arrived. I recall that I didn't know how to propose that he should come and edit the magazine, and so I asked Marcia [Leiseca], who was executive secretary of Casa at that time. When Retamar was told, he leapt up and said: "What I've dreamed of all my life, to create a literary journal!" And, of course, we didn't hold back because nothing should be left as it is born, everything has to grow and develop. And the Casa magazine also grew as the moment demanded.

Through that magazine, the continent's writers expressed themselves and explained what was happening from their points of view. It's a difficult magazine to produce because it is literary and political at the same time. It has been praised on many occasions and at other times criticized. But I believe that one of our characteristics is that we do not fear controversy. After all, controversy serves to measure our strengths. The [Cuban] Revolution is very strong, but it has to confront a powerful enemy: imperialism. And a controversial article doesn't get Cubans pulling their hair out. In many cases the writer of such an article will have a magnificent political position; maybe he or she doesn't share my point of view, but if it's interesting, we publish it and are confident that the debate it leads to will be a healthy one.

That's the way the magazine comes together; after compiling the contents, we work on other aspects. Mariano was already in charge of visual arts here at Casa; Galich in charge of drama; and the library is well underway. I believe it has to be a library specializing in the problems of our continent, able to serve academics both within and without. The library currently has more than 77,000 volumes, almost all devoted to Latin America.

For musical issues we have Argeliers León, a specialist. But a department of that nature poses a problem: we have to ask ourselves the question: What music? What is genuine Mexican music? And Peruvian? What is authentic Chilean or Venezuelan music? The problems of music are very broad. They are closely tied to human beings, because anyone who doesn't sing or dance at least moves, which is a well-known phenomenon — above all in Cuba, right? Now we are publishing the *Boletín de Música* and one day we'll have a magazine, in the not-so-distant future. Here we have had gatherings of musicians (and artists, theater people and writers). We have a project to release albums of Latin American music. But we have to ask ourselves again, what is authentic Latin American music? Musicologists themselves aren't even certain. We should be compiling what has been called folkloric music, and music with a content that, while not being folkloric, has very much its own roots. There has always been controversy over the albums we have released, whether or not they are genuinely Latin American, but without those controversies things would not be clarified.

If there is one pastime profoundly rooted in Haydée Santamaría — maybe more than a pastime, a daily and constant habit — it is reading. She still recalls the long hours of reading, sometimes until dawn, during her childhood and adolescence, not to mention the family reprimands over bedtime. She avidly read Les Misérables, The Count of Montecristo *and* The Three Musketeers. *She tells us that she used to read back then the way she reads today, untiringly. She regularly comments and exchanges opinions on books with those close to her or her collaborators. But out of all your reading, can you say what book most impressed you?*

That depends on the period. Anatole France's *Island of Penguins* impressed me greatly when I read it in prison; some years later I read it again and it didn't impress me as much. I believe that books impress you more or less according to the circumstances and the moment. For example, each time I read [José] Martí, I discover something new. I had his *Complete Works* in prison with me. I didn't even finish reading them. I pored over the second volume. I remember having read that Martí was in a gallery once and a particular painting impressed him greatly. In the margin of that paragraph I wrote: "Someday I won't be in a *galera* [women's prison] but in a gallery and I'll have to see that painting."

It is much later, the gray and chilly afternoon has set in. They are calling for Haydée, and she leaves the office. Through a half-open window we can see the white caps of the waves rising and breaking over the Malecón wall. Some sandwiches remained untouched on the table and, far from seeming tired, Haydée seemed even more animated. Despite the brusque change in temperature she hasn't touched her inhaler. Haydée came back. She brought us two cassettes, knowing that the spare we had might not be enough. And suddenly, I thought of Haydée as a combatant, of her unswerving will and disciplined spirit intermingled with her spontaneous and welcoming manner. Anyone who thinks that an interview with Haydée Santamaría will follow the traditional format of questions and answers has another thought coming. She vividly enters into the theme being discussed and exhausts it; but sometimes, suddenly, she will enrich it with the digression of an anecdote, a personal judgment or a humorous episode. If you interrupt her, you will undoubtedly deprive yourself of a vivid narration of our revolutionary history or possibly a lucid analysis of an artistic or literary figure of our world and our time. There were still two questions left on our agenda.

Every year some 600 to 700 works are sent in for the Casa Prize. There are 12 prizes now. If there is an unawarded dramatic piece that the jury [nevertheless] considers worthwhile producing, we send it to a theater group or groups in Cuba and Latin America so they can decide whether to stage it. In the case of work in other genres of a publishable quality, we send it to publishing houses with which we have relations and recommend those works to them. We have cooperated and want to continue cooperating because we haven't forgotten what our country was prior to the revolution.

The Cuban Revolution is a determining factor in Latin American literature, or at least for its dissemination. It is the revolution that is stimulating that interest, both in Latin America and in Europe. It was after the revolution that this desire to know the literature of our continent was aroused.

The interview is interrupted for a few minutes. We recalled Haydée's long-held admiration for Simón Bolívar, her devotion to Martí since the years of her rebellious childhood when she invented a Mambí grandfather and took flowers to his imaginary grave; or those ardent and innocent patriotic compositions to the national hero that she recited on Fridays in the little Encrucijada schoolhouse.

A few minutes ago you were telling us about the collection of popular Chilean art that you requested from President Salvador Allende and which he later sent to the Casa de las Américas. We know that collection is large, valuable and important and that, in addition to popular works of art, it contains paintings, sculptures and engravings from all over the continent. Could you tell us what the Casa de las Américas intends to do with that collection?

We've had that collection for many years. Starting with the concept that this continent is one and the same thing, we here at Casa felt that, Cuba being the country that it is, we have the most appropriate conditions for bringing together the art of the peoples. It is those less elaborate forms of genuine expression that fill me with passion. There are families of potters with a tradition dating back hundreds and hundreds of years. The works are not spontaneous or improvised. It is enough to see the popular art of those families in Puebla, Mexico, a couple of times to recognize their style. It also has function. Even the children make the dye, look for the clay and mix the two together. But giving the piece form by placing it in the kiln is a job reserved for the person in the family who knows what they're doing. And the results are marvelously crafted pieces. It is an eminently popular art that should be distinguished from what is "populist," using the term populist in its most pejorative sense. Popular means made by the people, and that which is assimilated by the peoples, with authenticity. The "populists" are those who want to commercialize art and, since that is the case, they go by what is in fashion — if the fashion is African or Japanese they make African or Japanese objects. The whole thing is a fraud because it is not genuine.

I fear that this popular Latin American art could gradually be extinguished for a host of reasons. There could be a rupture in a family tradition that has been passing down its knowledge from generation to generation over hundreds of years. That art form has to be conserved because it is a form of expression of the peoples of this continent. So, Cuba possesses this very important collection.

Mexico, Bolivia, Peru and Guatemala also have very good collections. But here we have pieces from all of those places and the rest of the continent, including the Amazon region. I don't know what we will call the venue housing that collection. We will have to find an appropriate name. That collection of more than 1,500 pieces will be here, not for Cuba alone but for the peoples of our continent. If the Casa de las Américas is capable of undertaking that task, one day that collection will be where this America decides, because that day we will be united as a people. For now, it has befallen Cuba to look after the collection and it will be the Casa de las Américas that undertakes that role. Will we be capable of doing so? I don't know.

Where would the collection be displayed?

It is difficult with so many pieces. The problem of space has arisen. Certain climatic conditions are required so that they don't deteriorate. Now that there is a Ministry of Culture we hope they will recognize the need for more space. It doesn't have to be huge. Apart from those pieces, we also have to remember that we cannot lose the paintings that make up this great collection, the finest in Latin America according to experts like Mariano, Soto — the Venezuelan painter — and Matta, the Chilean. They perceive it as a collection of works of great quality. Many valuable paintings by Latin American artists are dispersed in various countries. On the other hand, those who want to see a collection of all of them brought together are only going to find that in this country. It would be enough if the national museum, where there is a focus on collecting Cuban works, would lend us a small exhibition of the works of our painters so that Cuba is represented. Cuba would be the depository of all of those cultural values, but based on a continental criterion. And within 50 or 100 years this collection will be housed in the most appropriate country. It will be the responsibility of the upcoming generation and those after them, to care jealously for that collection, conserve it above all until this America is the real America: the one that Martí so desired.

On that note Haydée, how have your relations with writers and artists developed?

I feel that I can communicate with artists, both those with whom I work and see every day and those with whom I have had working relations in one way or another. It has been easy for me. When I began to direct the Casa de las Américas I maybe didn't have a very clear concept of what a writer or an artist was. I supposed that they had to be something of a snob, extravagant. And it has been here, in the Casa de las Américas, that I have learned to respect creators in the arts and literature and where, moreover, I do not allow any lack of respect for them, because I know that they are fighters, always restless. I have learned a lot from those *compañeros* that have worked in the Casa de las Américas for many years — like Mariano, Galich, Retamar, Lesbia, Peña, Benedetti, Benítez, Argeliers — all eminent figures in the arts and literature. They are my real advisers on aesthetic issues. At the same time, I have been able to offer them leadership. I think that they are able to absorb ideas and ways of being, maybe due to my having more information and being more up to date in the political context and from moving in areas that are not specifically theirs.

In that way, I would say that I have been a point of balance among the different artistic expressions: avoiding a preponderance of the visual arts over poetry, or music over drama.

And now, once again, comes the contradiction between the previous question and spontaneous responses: an interview with Haydée consists of various potential interviews, but that comes with the profession.

Returning to the theme of Casa, Haydée. You still haven't talked of the importance of the published works, the designs of those publications — some of them of excellent quality — or of the labors of the Literary Research Center (CIL) or the theater department.

Right. I believe that in relation to Latin America, Casa publications have an inestimable importance. We receive constant petitions from the universities in Cuba and other countries on the continent. The students need them, particularly those in humanities. So there is an attempt to make our literature known. Literature always reflects the life of peoples, and it was necessary to circulate those stories in Latin America and in other countries. Generally speaking, Latin American literature was unknown to the general public. It was little known in the socialist countries — with the exception of Vallejo, Neruda, Guillén and a few others. But they transcend Latin American literature, they have become universal. Through the Casa de las Américas — the publications, the prizes — Cuba has introduced the writers and the literature of our continent. For example, Victor Volski, director of the Latin American Institute of the Science Academy of the Soviet Union, was here recently and through people like him we have been able to circulate widely many of those works. *Bertillón 166*, Soler Puig's novel that won the prize in 1960, was translated into various languages in the socialist countries. Likewise, many of those that didn't receive awards have been translated. We have spoken about Latin American writers here with cultural attachés from the socialist countries. It is not an exaggeration to say that the Casa de las Américas has fulfilled an important role in circulating the continent's literature. And that's how it should be.

We have a design department that has been directed by Umberto Peña for the past 15 years, and, as you have said, some of our design has attained the highest quality. I think that this department's greatest creation has been its work during very difficult years in our country, when sometimes out of necessity, and at others, out of a lack of concern, graphic design was ignored. However, it was a fundamental task for our designers to attain the highest standard possible. They achieved the best with the few materials available. If a book's content was important for the editorial group, design was the major factor for the art department. By this I mean to say that it was always about coordinating the two things, because there was no contradiction in choosing between content and design.

On the other hand, I would say that our Literary Research Center (CIL) has done a great job. (Mario) Benedetti has worked hard to perform his job efficiently and effectively. When he had to leave Cuba, Trini (Trinidad Pérez), a very young *compañera*, replaced him. The CIL has only a few staff, but the *compañeros* there work with rigor. You should see how much research they have undertaken. Nobody knows how many things they have to do or how many people they have to consult or interview in order to carry out an investigation. Some university students have been with CIL for two or three years. Afterwards they are reclaimed by the system, because they are needed as professors. I have said that they must be allowed to go, because professors are very important. Moreover, I'm not just director of the Casa de las Américas, I feel a part of the whole revolutionary process, and have to take into consideration where people will be most useful or necessary.

Then we have relations with the Latin American theater movement. It is often thought that bringing a visiting theater group to the island is the most important thing for the theater movement, and that's not always the case. The *Conjunto* magazine comments on the work of Latin American groups and publishes its own works. In that way the groups and their forms and styles are assessed and information is circulated on what they're performing. It would be a much easier task just to bring over a theater group to perform three or four pieces in Cuba. Nevertheless, we would like to bring over groups. For example, there's a Mexican one, I think it's called Teatro-Café or Café-Teatro. It's composed of four or five actors and a high-quality singer and I believe it would be a great thing to present that group in our country.

Could you say more? How do you see the Casa de las Américas' perspectives within the framework of the country's institutionalization and the creation of the Ministry of Culture?

I can say that we are well established in our work, in what we have done and what we could do and I believe we should do a lot more. I think that the Ministry of Culture could give us a bit of a hand. Everyone has his or her hopes placed on the Ministry of Culture, which must not let us down. But neither can we expect miracles, and I'm not saying this because the Minister of Culture [Armando Hart] is my husband. And I can assure you that, from my own personal experience, he cannot work any miracles.

Casa de las Américas, November-December, 1988

part two: *light*

About Haydée

The Permanence of Haydée

Roberto Fernández Retamar

Just as the Casa de las Américas would not exist without Haydée, it is difficult to imagine it without Roberto Fernández Retamar. Director of the Casa magazine since 1965, and current director of the Casa de las Américas. A poet, essayist, teacher and scholar, Retamar founded the Union of Cuban Writers and Artists (UNEAC) in 1964 and in 1995 he presided over the jury of the 17th International Festival of New Latin American Film. In 1952 he won the National Prize for Poetry, and in both 1989 and 1996 he won the Cuban National Prize for Literature. Among his poems, "Elegía como un himno" (1950), "Patrias" (1952); "Vuelta de la antigua esperanza" (1959), "Buena suerte viviendo" (1967), "Juana y otros temas personales" (1981) and "Aquí" (1995), constitute some of the most important literary works in contemporary Cuban literature. One of the world's foremost scholars of José Martí, in 1977 he founded the Center for Martí Studies and served as its director until 1986. In addition, he has served as Cuba's Cultural Consul to France and as an elected member of the National Assembly of People's Power and as a member of the Council of State.

Given that I had one of the greatest privileges of my life to work under Haydée's personal direction and in close collaboration with her, there would be no sense in seeking new things to say about her. I had written a brief (unsigned) introduction to her personal account of the Moncada assault, published in 1967, as well as a brief biography. I dedicated one of my books to her, whose recent expanded edition is also for her. Another book she knew in its unpublished form and which led Silvia Gil, Haydée and myself to Nicaragua in February, I dedicated to her "clear and passionate memory," given that she has passed away. What she awoke in me during her life is what she continues to awake. When I began to spend time with her, despite her "lightning laughter," she already had the majesty of a great martyr; and now that she cannot hear us, she nevertheless seems more alive than many people.

One day, talking of trivial things (at least that's what I thought), Haydée suddenly asked me if I would speak at her graveside. She alarmed me, as she had a habit of doing. For a moment I had forgotten that, under or above the words she exchanged with us, she was always speaking with the dead that she carried within her, with death itself. I don't know whether, among the very many rural readings she did (often from clearing to clearing, like Don Quixote), she read Unamuno: I know she would have found the tormented Basque's agonized meditation on death natural. But I also have no doubts that she would have found more to her liking that other great woman of similar talent to Haydée's, known in her century as Teresa de Ahumada, and now as Santa Teresa de Jesús, who with a brother, read of feats of justice and dreams and tried to make them real, undertaking in her time what was renovating and valiant. Like the Cuban woman, while loving life to the full, Santa Teresa also desired death. It is known that Martí fervently read this indulgent mother of Avila. In 1905, aged just 21, Pedro Henríquez Ureña, the father of 20th century Latin American criticism, affirmed that at times Martí's style "has the emotional intensity of Teresa de Jésus," and 25 years later, added that Martí wrote "with the candor of Santa Teresa, from whom he learned that one who feels as he should does not have to hold back." In 1930, another indulgent mother, Gabriela Mistral, said of Martí: "Although the comparison seems absurd at first glance, one thinks of a Victor Hugo corrected of his exaggeration and of his trumpeting voice by a daily and educational relationship with the domestic and voluntarily popular Santa Teresa." Developing such observations in 1941, Juan Marinello, the unforgettable communist maestro, dedicated profound pages to what he called "the Teresa" in Martí, stressing similarities between the Spanish woman and the Cuban man in aspects such as mysticism, "a pleasure in suffering," "desiring death" and the "intimate tragedy of love dressed in uniform."

This undoubted side of Martí was another reason, a new and heartfelt reason for Haydée to identify so strongly with him. Not everyone who admires Martí, including many very eminent comrades, has shared certain facets of our national hero, like that "desire for death" revealed both in intimate pages and in many public texts written or spoken throughout his brief and electrifying life. From an early age, Martí went about "courting death," as Antonio Machado says of García Lorca's road to martyrdom. The examples are striking and one recalls that line in *Versos Sencillos*: "I tasted once, that fate / a taste like no other: when / the sentence of my death, was read out by the weeping governor." This verse immediately recalls the well-known poem by Santa Teresa in which she repeats like a sounding bell the verse: "I die because I do not die." Or that exclamation "close to the premonitory end," as Marinello said: "Death is jubilation, renewal, a new task. Death! Generous death! Death my friend!" These are the closest I can get today to the words that Haydée, shocking me, asked me to say over her grave.

I think that I have never, and far less in circumstances like these, wanted to be original in the sense of the novel: what I have wanted and still do is to be faithful to the original, which is very different. And in the case of Haydée, her origins go back to the very soul of the nation: the little nation, Cuba, and the great nation, "Our America," as Martí named us.

Haydée's life took off in a little place in the center of Cuba, and advanced to the center of history: the assaults of July 26, 1953, those events that Fidel expressed so well in *History Will Absolve Me* [Fidel Castro's courtroom defense of the Moncada trial]:

> The air of the glorious epic can still be felt in Oriente at dawn,
> when the cocks sing like bugles sounding the reveille to the
> soldiers and the sun rises radiant over the soaring moun-
> tains; every day seems like those of Yara or Baire [historic
> moments in Cuba's independence struggle from Spain].

In a dedication that she showed me one luminous afternoon, the
poet Cintio Vitier, who profoundly understood her as he has understood so many things about Cuba, had told Haydée that he
"always saw her in the founding dawn." Thus, she lived the rest
of her life at that moment of glory and supreme pain in which
Yara and Baire burned once again. And knowing facts about her
life before that date we can understand that in some apparently
blind way — but in reality guided by a rare compass — Haydée
had set about preparing herself for that terrible and stunning
encounter with history. We have some facts from her childhood
she evidently told Melba Hernández, her sister in struggle and
hope — perhaps told her during those days and nights in prison
— and which Melba conserved and passed on as the treasures
that they are.

Although I don't intend to reevoke all the details of her life,
certain aspects cannot be left out. As a child, when she wanted
to be a mother like one of the hens from her house, and for that
subjected herself to the bird's angry pecking. And, some years
later, being the daughter of Spaniards, inventing for herself a
Mambí [freedom fighter] grandfather after a teacher in the little
school attached to the sugar mill taught her how our country had
been forged. The adolescent who rejected without hesitation the
maneuvers of the local *cacique*, the girl who suffered over the
assassination of Jesús Menéndez, the great communist labor
leader in the area. And the young woman, sickened by the sewer
of the neocolonial republic and drawn by Eddy Chibás's implacable exposé of it and his slogan "Shame on Money," joined the
ranks of the Orthodox youth with her brother Abel and moved
toward the flame from which would arise the decisive stage in a

process of liberation already more than 100 years old.

I talked with her on various occasions about the struggle against the military coup of March 10, 1952, her meeting up with Fidel, the preparations for what was to be July 26, the "founding dawn." In the first place and, as always with the moral authority he had to do so, comrade Fidel talked of Haydée's conduct born of the assault and the massacre in those indelible lines from *History Will Absolve Me*.

At that time, Haydée not only knew that she had lost the brother of her soul and her fiancé in a horrific way, but had no knowledge as to whether Fidel himself was alive. She was alone with Melba facing the horror, forced to dredge strength from her insides. She found that strength, as if in an unknown part of herself. That girl would never be the same as before and, nonetheless, had returned in a unique form. But Moncada, as it is known, was not only a military battle: it was also a juridical battle and — above all — a political battle. Although the military battle, followed by atrocious butchery, ended in defeat for the assailants, the other two battles signified definitive triumphs. The reverse side of weaponry began to reveal a victorious face. That was the reason for the tremendous importance of the assailants' trial, thanks to which the accused became the valiant and implacable accusers of the regime. In this combat and its supreme culmination in *History Will Absolve Me*, Haydée played a fundamental role. A survivor of the massacres, a witness to the torture that tore her dearest from her in a horrific manner, her declaration was definitive.

At the end of the trial, Haydée and Melba were sentenced to seven months' imprisonment. Of course, prison was hard for them. Prior to the formal sentencing they had been placed with common prisoners, with the idea that the latter would make life difficult for them. But those criminals were more caring and tender with them than the others, those bloody criminals who had snatched power [in the 1952 coup]. And with the formidable words of all the comrades in the trial, the insurrectional process had gained even more heart, and they knew the tasks assigned to them after their release. Hours of reading filled the days of that "university of the revolutionary" which is prison. While Fidel did the same in his cell on the Isle of Pines, in the Guanajay prison Haydée re-read and commented on Martí's complete works; the volumes with her girlish writing in the margins have been preserved.

By 1954 they were released. Their first mission was to circulate clandestinely the *Mensaje a Cuba que Sufre* [*Message to a Suffering Cuba*], a manifesto in which Fidel explained to the people how their brothers were brutally murdered. And soon, the most important mission: to publish and distribute *History Will Absolve Me*, reconstructed by Fidel and sent out of the prison sheet by sheet. Thousands of copies flooded the country and even reached abroad.

The following year, after an intensive popular campaign, Fidel, Raúl, Almeida, Ramiro, Montané and the other survivors were released. "It was like living again," Haydée said. A dramatic photo captures the moving reencounter: Haydée leaning her head against Fidel's chest, after her desperate eyes had sought him out among the radiant faces of those emerging.

With Fidel out on the streets, the process was unstoppable. The vanguard had a mentor: Martí, and a guide: Fidel. It already had a name, a watchword: the July 26 Movement, with Haydée on its national directorate. When Fidel left for Mexico to organize what would become the *Granma* expedition, Haydée went underground, using the name *María*.

At the end of 1956, awaiting the imminent arrival of the *Granma* cabin cruiser, Haydée traveled to Santiago de Cuba. She was among the organizers of the uprising in that city on November 30, shortly before the landing that rocked the island. Having withdrawn to a mansion when the final shoot-out ended, Haydée recalled the fateful hours in the hospital bordering the Moncada Garrison, where she was arrested with Abel, Melba, Raúl Gómez García and other comrades on July 26, 1953. They couldn't stay in the mansion and had to try to escape by any means. And they did. New comrades were with her, including two magnificent young people from Santiago: Frank País (*David*) and Vilma Espín (*Débora*); as well as a restless lawyer she knew in the underground movement and whom she had married a few months earlier: Armando Hart, code-named *Jacinto*.

Their married life was of course hazardous. Hart, who had led a spectacular escape from the hearing in Havana, was as much wanted by the police as she was. In the cities, they could only see each other for a few days in one house or another, between one mission and another. They also met up at times in the Sierra Maestra, where Haydée reencountered intimate friends like Fidel and Celia Sánchez, and came to know others: including the man with whom she exchanged banter and medicine to counter asthma: Che Guevara. On one of those occasions, descending from the Sierra on a mission, Hart was arrested and imprisoned on the Isle of Pines after a dangerous odyssey. Shortly afterwards, the Movement's directorate sent Haydée abroad on difficult tasks that she successfully accomplished.

When the revolution came to power on January 1, 1959, Haydée, who had returned to Cuba, was appointed director of the recently created Casa de las Américas. At last she could also have a home, where she gave birth to two children, and into which she would take other children from Our America.

With the merging of the revolutionary organizations Haydée, as a former member of the July 26 national directorate, moved to the national directorate of the United Party of the Socialist Revolution. And on October 3, 1965, that unforgettable night when Fidel, after announcing the constitution of the Central Committee of the Communist Party of Cuba, made public in his voice the farewell letter Che left with him when he departed for "other lands of the world," Haydée's name was naturally there, with her position ratified until her death, as was her presence on the Council of State.

When I said that Haydée's origins also date back to the very soul of the great homeland of Our America, as could be imagined, I thought of the fact that the revolution had assigned the unhesitating follower of José Martí, the sisterly comrade of Fidel and Che (all of them rooted in the continent) exceedingly important Latin American responsibilities. What the Casa de las Américas has done and how it has always met its basic guidelines is well known. Following Haydée's impassioned and lucid orientations, Casa has fulfilled the essential task of affirming, defending and circulating the genuine values of Our America. In a similar spirit Haydée presided over the Latin American Solidarity Conference (OLAS) which took place in Havana from July 31 through August 10, 1967.

Those of us who had the honor to participate in it will never forget Haydée's dynamic and feverish activity prior to and throughout the conference. Neither will we forget that when the curtain opened on the first day a huge effigy of the liberator Simón Bolívar appeared in the background and, in the final session, the effigy was of Che, who was fighting in the front line of what was at that time a new Bolivarian army.

So many recollections pile up when evoking the years spent with Haydée. How wonderful (I have said it before, like many of these things) to have seen and heard that woman of the people talking with numerous writers and artists from Our America, for whom she was always the mirror in the Chinese fable: the mediocre cannot recognize greatness, for such recognition is reserved for the great: great in soul, of course. I will confine myself to one example among the many that could be adduced. I have known few humans as refined, talented, honest and upstanding as Julio Cortázar. And what a spectacle to have been present at the dialogue between the dazzling Haydée and that dazzling Argentine. A dialogue that often seemed more like a monologue, because the master of fascinating words preferred to listen, fascinated, awed at the flow of the inexhaustible conversation that gushed forth from that woman, a conversation where the stones of every day crossed with the lightning bolts of a Sybil. (The edition of *Casa* magazine dedicated to Julio on his death contained a large number of admirable pages that he had sent to Haydée.)

Given that some lines back I recalled the OLAS conference and Che's epic struggle in Bolivia, I also want to bring to this testimony an afternoon in October 1967. I had met with Haydée in Casa de las Américas to talk about certain issues concerning the magazine. When we had exhausted those themes, I asked her about the possible truth of the worldwide cable reports of Che's death. I supposed, I told her, that the news must be false, like so many referring to us over so many years. Haydée didn't reply. As if she was a child, the child she never ceased to be, she burst into floods of tears. She didn't even make the effort to cover her face with her hands. I had to put my handkerchief over it myself. And after a while she began to mutter: "Abel, Frank, Che: I can't take it any more." It was as if she knew how to shape my blurred words into lines that seemed to flow from that Saint Teresa of Avila. Naturally, I refer to the letter she sent that same month to a shadow, to a light, which appeared on the first page of an edition that *Casa* magazine dedicated to the hero. [The letter by Haydée to Che is reprinted in Part One of this volume].

For reasons of time I am forced to make a big leap and arrive at the interminable night that began in the afternoon of July 28, 1980, and ended in the afternoon of the following day. That night, when I entered in desolation the funeral parlor where Haydée's body was laid out, I found the workers from the Casa de las Américas, headed by that band of women I have seen grow older, along with many, many other comrades, perplexed, vacant. Among those of us who were then working in Casa there was one for whom without any doubt Haydée felt the greatest affection: one day she told me that he reminded her of her father. That comrade, who was not only a notable artist who had accompanied

José Lezama Lima in his cultural task of resistance and creation, but was also proud of his own life as a revolutionary dating back to his adolescence, presented a rough exterior, perhaps due we thought to his harsh Canary Islands' descent; that comrade, Mariano, of course, was bathed in tears, something that was all the more impressive in someone as solid as an oak, and bathed in tears he remained until the last moment. "Nothing is more sad than a Titan weeping," wrote Rubén Darío. But who didn't cry that night? Dearest Arquímides patted someone on the back in consolation, unaware that he was crying himself; and the poet Eliseo embraced a man almost the same age as himself, mumbling: "My son." That night various hands put together this statement from the Executive Committee of the Casa de las Américas:

> We are writing these words in the midst of one of the greatest griefs of our lives; these words that, for the first time in many years, Haydée Santamaría will not be able to read before they go to press, to give her opinion on this or that idea, to ask for a word to be softened that could hurt a friend, to observe with unusually bright eyes the chink or error that had escaped others. As in all such cases, it seems inconceivable to us that her name, so fragrant and beautiful, is no longer that of a living person. But, as in those extremely rare cases, we have the certainty that her transit though existence was that of an exceptional creature, who possessed something of the volcano and the flower, the beauty of a cyclone or a dawn in the mountain, the unusual capacity of combating with love, of loving with the terrible intensity of combat.
>
> Others knew the privilege of being with her in the Moncada attack, in the Sierra or in the underground struggle. She was already a sacred figure in our history when the revolution charged her with creating the Casa de las Américas. And with the same passion, the same fire and the same tenderness that she put into everything, she made the Casa de las Américas, of which she was both the brains and the heart. When she could no longer be the guerrilla that in some ways she

never ceased to be, she earned the respect and love of writers and artists from all of Our America.

The most creative among them, the most imaginative and most faithful, understood her. They understood and listened with devotion to that countrywoman who did not go to college or to any institute. They knew that she was accompanied by paintings, transfixed by music, because she had an artist's sensibility. That sensibility took her to the revolution, and she brought to the revolution hundreds and thousands of men and women. As in certain heartrending verses by Mistral, which in Haydée's case acquire new meaning, "she wore her whole heart on her sleeve."

Only by being outside of herself could she have destroyed her own life. More than anyone, Haydée knew that her life did not belong to her, that it belonged to the revolution, to the people of that America of ours whose evocation misted her eyes and lit up her soul. It is necessary to say that she will be with us, within us. That is how it is. But from this moment we are the poorer without her, even though the honor of having worked under her guidance, under her encouragement — that we continue to feel at our side, proudly and intimately moved — will accompany us for ever.

Five years later, the *Casa* magazine once more dedicated an editorial to Haydée from which these lines are taken:

On July 28, 1980, the last of the revolutionaries tortured on account of the assault on the Moncada Garrison 27 years previously, died as the result of that torture. On that day Haydée Santamaría handed over what remained of her life. That is the way it was perceived by her great friends. In July 1953, they wounded her to death: not with bullets, but with evil, to quote from her deeply beloved Martí. Will it be necessary today to reevoke that evil, those "blows like the hatred of God," as Vallejo said? ... But the "wounds of Moncada," as *compañero* Juan Almeida expressed it, "never managed to heal in her." On the contrary: even in the midst of victory, of joy, of creation, of new and stimulating battles, they remained open like a chasm which finally devoured her, dragging her into a psychiatric illness from which one can also die, as one dies in armed combat or is eaten away by other physical diseases that did not spare Haydée. From the shadows that were initially cast in 1953 emerged the hand that murdered her in 1980. Was it her own? Or was it not rather one of those bestial hands that castrated fiancés or pulled out the eyes of brothers, alive, and sowed in a valiant, pure, strong and fragile girl a seed that later sullied her reason?

Those who saw that in her striding, day by day, in her last moments, without knowing it, like a character from a tragedy, toward a gallows inexorably awaiting her in the past; her *compañeros* on so many fronts and among them those of Casa to which she gave birth like another baby, proud and grateful for everything that she taught us, inconsolable on account of the illness — not herself, who by then virtually did not exist — that took her from us, once again pay her our emotional homage, by bringing here pages of her, or on her, created with truth and beauty by some of her uncountable comrades in struggle and by some of those no less countable dreamers who had the privilege of having her around them.

During her life, but especially after her death, splendid texts have been published on Haydée, giving reason to the words of the woman most identified with her in Casa, because she entered its building almost at the same time of its founding: Marcia Leiseca. Speaking on the 20th anniversary of the *Casa de las Américas* magazine, Marcia said:

> Haydée: there will never be any meeting, event or anniversary of this, your Casa, in which your luminous image is not present with us. Your life as an indomitable guerrilla of Moncada, of the Sierra, of the plains and in exile is part of our history. Your personality will be recreated by artists and converted for our children and future generations into a beautiful legend,

one of those dazzling myths that the peoples enrich in their imagination.

For us, Haydée was part of our daily life. Her light and swift step, her monologues, her permanent rebellion, her speech at times vague and unhurried, her gaze lost in a horizon we were unable to reach, her overflowing imagination, her infinite tenderness and the exuberance of her thinking and language were all natural to us. Through these and other traits we glimpsed that nothing in her was gratuitous, because on clearing the way we always learned a profound truth or a fact of the most genuine justice. We had the privilege of knowing her intimately, of loving her, of sharing a stage in the life of this exceptional being made for great things, for the purest and noblest passions, for growing in the most difficult situations or on account of the most delicate and complex problems.

Her passion for art surged spontaneously from her extraordinary sensibility, from her Martí training and from her fervor and love for Our America. She had the gift of a real leader: being capable of bringing out the best qualities in everyone. That allowed her to be part of a team in which mediocrity never flourished but, on the contrary, grew the finest flowers of the human condition. She brought together that force and with her this Casa was created day by day, slowly, sowing achievements and rectifying errors.

It can be and should be said that the relevance of Haydée's work is revealed in that of the entire Cuban Revolution but with particular intensity in her original creation that is the Casa de las Américas, which is growing and spreading within the dream with which she created it; in that Casa where her rebellious, imaginative and ingenious spirit survives. Haydée would soon have reached her 80th birthday. How hard it is to believe that. In the revolution and in Casa, she remains forever young.

In the Face of Haydée's Death

Juan Almeida

A founding member of the July 26 Movement, Juan Almeida is one of the few remaining Moncada combatants, Isle of Pines prisoners, and members of the Granma expedition that brought the revolutionaries to Cuba's shores in 1956. In the Sierra Maestra he was promoted to the rank of Commander of the Santiago de Cuba Column of the Rebel Army. Almeida has served as both Chief of the Air Force and Chief of the Army among many other positions. Currently, he is a member of the Political Bureau of the Central Committee of the Communist Party of Cuba, Vice-President of the Council of State, and President of the Association of Combatants of the Cuban Revolution.

Dear *compañeros,*

There is no more painful and sorrowful duty than that which falls upon us this afternoon.

We have come here to bid farewell to an impassioned combatant of our revolution from the most distant and difficult days; to an intimate and beloved comrade of us all and all the people; to a figure of incalculable international prestige who, through her merits and consistent labor became an outstanding representative of revolutionary Cuba's heroism, history, spirit of struggle and sentiment of solidarity.

In her own right, Haydée Santamaría occupies an indelible place in the Cuban Revolution. For that reason the circumstances that led to her death are doubly bitter.

Haydée was one of us who, from the March 10 [1952] coup onwards, began to search for a new way for Cuba's redemption, and we found it at Fidel's side. When we still had nothing, no arms, no money, and no public renown; when we had virtually nothing other than our dreams and our desire to fight, together with her brother Abel she became a central support of the revolutionary movement that was being born. As we know, she participated in the assault on the Moncada Garrison, and there she resisted with an unassailable fortitude one of the hardest tests to have befallen any revolutionary, when the dictatorship's henchmen tormented her with the bloody remains confirming their savage murder of Abel and other equally beloved and intimate comrades. She was familiar with prison. She left it with comrade Melba to devote herself completely to the orientations and tasks drawn up by comrade Fidel from prison, directed at reorganizing the revolutionary movement, which included the first edition and distribution of *History Will Absolve Me.*

As an underground fighter she participated with Frank País and other combatants in organizing the November 30 [1956] uprising in Santiago de Cuba [when the urban underground of the July 26 Movement organized an uprising in the city to divert the attention of Batista's troops away from the imminent landing of the *Granma.* Unfortunately, the *Granma* was delayed due to bad weather and difficult sea conditions and did not arrive until three days later], as well as many other tasks in the island's cities. From its foundation, she was a member of the July 26 Movement's National Directorate. She was part of the Rebel Army insurrection in the Sierra Maestra, despite health problems, and remained in the mountains for some time until, on Fidel's orders, she traveled abroad to fulfill important revolutionary missions. Wherever she was, she always maintained a total dedication to the cause, revolutionary stoicism and an obsession for struggle always characterized her.

After the January 1 [1959] victory she dedicated herself with a singular spirit to the country's new tasks. She spared no effort in the consolidation and advance of our socialist homeland. She was a bulwark of our party, and was a member of the Central Committee from its constitution. And her labor of 20 years at the head of the Casa de las Américas constitutes an exceptional contribution to the friendship, solidarity, culture and development of unbreakable ties between Cuba and its sister nations in Latin America, the Caribbean and other parts of the world, and to the example and truth of Cuba struggling victoriously against the blockade and calumnies of U.S. imperialism, and against the continent's fascists and reactionaries.

As revolutionaries we cannot agree on principle with suicide. The life of a revolutionary belongs to his or her cause and people and should be devoted to serving them to the last ounce of energy and the last second of existence. But we cannot coldly judge comrade Haydée. That would not be just.

Those of us who knew her well were aware that the wounds of the Moncada attack never finally healed in her. But above all, in more recent years, comrade Haydée suffered a progressive deterioration in her health. In addition to this, a few months ago she was involved in a car accident that almost took her life, and which further aggravated both her physical and psychological state. Only these circumstances — which no doubt took her to the extreme of losing hold of herself — can explain why a figure of her historic and revolutionary rank, with such high merits before the nation and socialism, whose spirit was put to the test at the most difficult and heroic moments of our struggle — was consumed with the tragic decision to take her own life.

For that reason, this painful end cannot diminish her virtues, or the force of her revolutionary example, or the legacy that she has left to our new generations and, especially, to Cuban women.

We shall not remember her in her tragic final moment. We shall remember her alongside Abel and Fidel in the preparations for the revolutionary movement. We shall remember her as a heroine of Moncada. We shall remember her as a combatant in the Sierra and in the plains. We shall remember her as a constructor of our new homeland. We shall remember her in her example of combativeness, exertion, simplicity and total dedication to the cause of socialism and internationalism. And that example will be a source of renewed energy for those of us who must continue moving forward, fulfilling our duty to the homeland and the revolution.

Dear *compañeros*, on behalf of Haydée Santamaría's family, the Central Committee of the Party, the Council of State and the directorate of the Casa de las Américas, we express to you our most profound gratitude for having accompanied us at this time of grief.

Thank you very much.

Haydée: Fire and Light

Carlos Rafael Rodríguez

Renowned writer, journalist and economist as well as Cuba's deputy prime minis-
ter, Carlos Rafael Rodríguez was a Political Bureau member of the pre-revol-
utionary Cuban Communist Party.

Among the many positions he held following the 1959 revolution were editor-
in-chief of Hoy *newspaper, director of the University of Havana Economics*
Faculty, president of the National Institute for Agrarian Reform (INRA),
President of the National Commission for Economic and Scientific and Techni-
cal Cooperation, and Cuba's permanent representative on the Council for Mutual
Economic Assistance.

Recalling Haydée is like contemplating a flash of lightning, hearing
the crackling of burning forests. That is her image within us. Not
of sterile serenity but of flaming movement. Fire and light.

We began to get to know each other one day in 1957, her
eyes filling when we talked of Jesús Menéndez, the black worker
[and labor movement leader] of her early youth in her native Encrucijada. Years later, I saw her express herself with the same passion, but never more than when we lost Che. And one July 25,
20 years after the Moncada assault, I discovered that the joy of
the obvious achievements that justify the death of heroes had
not been able to cure her of the great distress that was still tear-
ing her apart.

She brought her burning passion to everything she did, at the
Moncada, in the [Communist] Party and in the Casa [de las

Américas], her enduring work. She launched herself into speaking like someone unleashing a whirlwind, as if the words didn't rise from her mind, which she used so well, but burst forth like Unamuno from the recesses of her soul... She was never argumentative, although she certainly reasoned with lucidity — but without fighting. Hearing her talk of literature, of art, failing to understand her analysis more than once, one recalled that supremely accurate description of culture not as an accumulation of data but as the internal expression of a way of seeing things. She didn't need a university degree or one from the Academy — which we never renounced, despite their frequently infertile fruits — to talk of the Greeks, of Michelangelo or of Picasso. She handled them with wisdom, an intuitive comprehension, which also framed many of her lively political opinions on the complex problems of revolutionary creativity.

She remains among us, we always sense her fire and her light. We hear the crackling of the tree trunks and the gentle murmur of her tender words.

March 12, 1985

Some Memories...

Melba Hernández

Along with Haydée, Melba Hernández was one of only two women who participated in the attack on the Moncada Garrison in 1953 that started Cuba's revolutionary war. A founding member of the July 26 Movement and the Cuban Communist Party, Hernández has been a member of the Party's Central Committee since 1986. With a Ph.D. in Law and a Master's degree in Social Sciences she has held many vital positions including: delegate to the National Assembly of People's Power, President of the Cuban Committee in Solidarity with South Vietnam, Cambodia and Laos, Vice-President of the Cuban Movement for Peace and Sovereignty of the People, Cuba's Ambassador to the Socialist Republic of Vietnam, and General Secretary of the Organization of Solidarity with the Peoples of Asia, Africa and Latin America (OSPAAAL).

Many things could be said of Yeyé, as those of us who were her family and most intimate friends called Haydée Santamaría. Memories come in floods and sometimes I smile at them as if we were seated facing each other like we used to do; others, inevitably, generate a state of mind that is difficult to overcome.

In an abstract sense, Yeyé — who in a very short period of time became a comrade, friend, sister, mother and daughter — through her political acumen and revolutionary fiber revealed herself as someone possessed of great humanity. Let me recall what she told me of her early years. When she was still a little girl, dolls weren't sufficient as objects of her maternal tenderness, and one day this child, who lived on a sugar plantation, could not be found. Despite her family's searching, they gave her up for lost in the depths of the sugar mill. When evening fell, her grand-father, crying secretly at the back of the house, heard some little sobs, went in their direction and found his little granddaughter lying in the nest of a hen that was just ready to lay her eggs. The child was bleeding from the peckings of the hen reclaiming the nest that Haydée, obstinately, refused to give up. On seeing her grandfather crying she told him that she was there because she too wanted to have little ones like the hen. Despite her tremendous courage and determination, even as an adult I sometimes saw her become insignificant when she had to face a cock or a hen.

That humanity was always evident in her care for her brother Abel, who was both a baby for her and a man that she was bound to with respect, obedience and admiration. It isn't easy to stifle the memories of that sister as she said goodbye to her bro-ther, here in Havana, when he left for an unknown destination; all the risks involved in the revolutionary struggle and the uncertainty as to whether she would see him again or not. That humanity was manifest, very evident, in the heat of the battle in the Saturnino Lora hospital in Santiago de Cuba on July 26 [1953]. Yeyé threw herself furiously into her task; she never let up her efforts to en-sure that nothing happened to Abel or me; she wanted to run all the risks, she wanted to save us with her own life and exposed herself to danger, running to the aid of the enemy who fell bleeding and dead.

For me she was also the dearly beloved sister that I never had, my comrade and friend, while at the same time I felt she was my little daughter, though she always tried to mother me. We were very happy, and in that period of the pre-Moncada strug-gle, in which discipline, respect, discretion and a close sisterhood with our comrades prevailed, we never lost the chance to go to any party we might hear about; we carried out our revolutionary tasks, combined with festive moments, with a youthful joy. We were kept in line by the combined voices of Abel and my mother, and constantly reminded of the responsibility of revolutionary undertakings by the voices of Fidel and Abel.

Now I would like to do for her what she tried to do for her brother Abel: I want Yeyé here today — alive — as an example for Latin American women, who still have a long way to go in the service of Our America's freedom and independence; for what she could do alongside them in solidarity with the struggle of our continent; and for the Cuban women whom she epitomized with such a beautiful image representing the nation's proud ideals; for her intelligence that, projected into work, gave rise to that respected and beloved labor of our Casa de las Américas. Finally, Yeyé is not dead — she is alive and will live on eternally in all those who know that happiness is only found when we give ourselves to the great endeavor on behalf of the peoples, on behalf of humanity.

The Presence and Absence of Haydée Santamaría

Mario Benedetti

Benedetti, world-renowned Uruguayan poet, essayist and novelist has published more than 70 works. Among them, a collection of his poems, Inventario e Inventario Dos, *short stories,* La muerte y otras sorpresas *(1968),* Con y sin nostalgia *(1977) and* Geografías *(1984), and novels,* Gracias por el fuego *(1965) and* Primavera con una esquina rota. *Between 1945 and 1973, he helped to develop and sustain the famous and outspoken Uruguayan political weekly,* Marcha. *Persecuted for his political beliefs, Benedetti was forced into exile in 1973. He spent the next 12 years in Argentina, Peru, Spain and Cuba. While in Cuba, he worked with Haydée at the Casa de las Américas.*

One month of July when various deaths of internationally known figures accumulated in press headlines (pianist José Iturbi, Indira Gandhi's son, comedian Luis Sandrini, Bolivian leader Quiroga Santa Cruz, actor Peter Sellers, Spanish politician Garrigues Walker, the former Shah of Iran, etc.), the death of Haydée Santamaría — at least in Europe — was probably reduced to a note, a footnote or a brief commentary from some news agency. But in Latin America the repercussions were shattering.

She was a combatant in the assault on the Moncada Garrison in another July — that of 1953 — *compañera* of Fidel Castro and Che Guevara in the revolutionary action in the Sierra Maestra and, after the triumph of the revolution in 1959, director of the

Casa de las Américas (a position she held to her death). She was likewise a member of the Central Committee of the Communist Party of Cuba and the Council of State. Despite that impressive curriculum vitae, and despite being one of the three celebrated heroines of the Cuban Revolution (the other two being Celia Sánchez — who had died a few months previously — and Vilma Espín), she was a figure who only appeared in public on very special occasions and who preferred to avoid protocol and the inevitable formalities that, under any regime, seem to be inherent in high political or state responsibilities. For that reason, I think that at the end of the day, the discretion with which, at least in Europe, her final combat, her last assault on death was transmitted, would not have caused much notice.

I am certain, however, that the news must have profoundly moved all those who, in some way, worked for Latin American culture, whether in their own countries or from exile. For painters, musicians, writers, singers, theater performers from Argentina or Venezuela, from Chile or Mexico, from Uruguay or Nicaragua, from Jamaica or El Salvador, and of course in her native Cuba, the very mention of Haydée Santamaría signifies a world, an attitude, a sensibility, and also a revolution, which she did not conceive of as confined to the land of José Martí but extended to the future of all our peoples.

In that Casa de las Américas of which she was the body and soul, I had the privilege of working with Haydée for many years, and as late as June of that year (1980), when she was convalescing from one of her increasingly more frequent circulatory crises, I was able to visit her at her home and have one of our many conversations, without knowing it was to be our last. It was evident that she wasn't well. After the extremely grave automobile accident she suffered in 1979, her health clearly had failed. Nevertheless, she continued to be an untiring conversationalist as always, attacking and defending causes with all her passion, which was not insignificant; at times giving the impression of an implacable rigor, but immediately returning to the constant generosity that was her style.

I have known few people as concerned to be fair as she was. Her confidence in people was infinite, and she always resisted judging others.

She had lived in burning proximity to death, which in the far-off times of the insurrectional struggle had taken many of her nearest and dearest. At the end of the day, for that reason it doesn't make very much difference if, on this July 28 — just 48 hours after the 27th anniversary of the Moncada assault — it was she who sought death, or if it was death that sought her. After all, they were well acquainted and it is even possible that they respected each other as formidable opponents.

Although Haydée had a great sense of humor, although she often openly roared with laughter, I am not convinced she was a genuinely happy being. Rather, I believe that she felt a profound need for happiness, and only the incessant search for that happiness could rescue her from her abyss of sadness. And after all, what was her thousand-times proven revolutionary militancy but a direct and dangerous form of attaining happiness, through gaining justice and dignity for human beings?

She wasn't a writer or a painter or a musician or an actress, but she had an unusual sensibility for grasping art and enjoying it. She alone had read more books than all of us writers who worked in the Casa de las Américas. And when the jurists arrived for the Casa Prize, she took it upon herself to remind them, so that there wouldn't be any misunderstanding: "Don't worry too much about awarding works that are politically impeccable; just concern yourselves with giving the prize to the best. And never forget that the prize is a literary one."

In a period when nobody knew or sponsored them, Haydée was an active promoter of the Cuban Nueva Trova [New Song] singers, like Silvio Rodríguez, Pablo Milanés and all the others who now attract huge audiences. The amplitude and comprehension with which this women, who wasn't an artist and did not try to be one, approached artistic matters, was simply exemplary. And with that attitude she came to fulfill an undeniable political function. When in 1961, the economic (and also cultural) U.S. blockade attempted to isolate Cuba from the other nations of Latin America, Haydée clearly understood that the Casa de las Américas could win out — clearly not over the economic blockade, but certainly over the cultural one. And so, instead of trying to create links with official institutions that were evidently going to follow the attitude of their respective governments, she made connections with writers and artists as individuals, as well as beings embedded in their communities. And the writers and artists responded to this Latin American calling and the daring proposal thus received a committed response.

So, for all those workers in Latin American culture, for all those loyal contributors to the Casa de las Américas, Haydée's death didn't strike them as a news item at the bottom of a page but with a sad and close-felt resonance. When Fidel Castro relates Haydée's dialogue with her hangmen in October 1953 in his famous defense plea, he makes this comment: "The name of Cuban womanhood was never placed on such a high pedestal of heroism and dignity." What was exceptional about this exceptional woman was that, once the revolution was won, she knew how to adjust her firm tread as a combatant to the urgent cultural needs not just of Cuba but of Latin America as a whole.

One day someone should analyze how her vision of this racially mixed continent greatly contributed to mutual comprehension and knowledge among Latin American artists. Many people will write, now and later and with every right, on her style of work. But at this moment, while the bald news of her death continues to weigh so heavily, I want to finally highlight that trait of hers which, through so many years of living alongside each other, of comradeship and shared labor, most profoundly impressed me: her generosity, which was as invincible as her courage. By whatever strange connections, that attribute is what most moves me in relation to this death. At the end of the day, her greatly admired Martí had already expressed it: "A good soul on earth hurts very much!"

What Can I Say About Haydée?

Alicia Alonso

Cuba's prima ballerina, Alicia Alonso studied ballet in Havana, New York and London. She has been the director and prima ballerina of the National Ballet of Cuba since the triumph of the revolution in 1959. Now partially blind, Alonso has won numerous awards including the Decoration of Carlo Mendez de Céspedes (1947), Dance Magazine Award (1958), Médaille de la Ville de Paris and Prix Pavlova (1966).

What can I say about Haydée, the heroine, the combatant, the revolutionary, when others have already spoken with such eloquence and love; and when she herself said it all with her life, with her presence so dearly beloved by all? I prefer to recall Haydée in details that might seem more trivial, but really are not, because they tell us much about her as a person and also define for us her grandeur and humanity.

I knew her personally in the first months after the triumph of the revolution, and very soon discovered in her a great sensibility, united with her frankness and simplicity. From that moment until the last day we saw each other, I felt that both of us could communicate. Haydée always rapidly understood what I proposed to her and even took it upon herself to clarify to others, at times with a polemical passion, the most intricate details of my point of view. I always noticed this and it was the reason why, like so many other artists, I began to see in her an important moral support for my work. She was a person who inspired strength and spirit, and above all, transmitted a great principle of honesty toward the revolution. We could talk to her for hours on end, and always wanted to go on listening to her. She had a totally unique way of analyzing problems and of focusing on any theme under discussion.

Her way of expressing ideas was unexpected but, nevertheless, in her own way she got to the truth, to the essence of things. She had a very idiosyncratic way of approaching any problem, whether it was cultural, political or an unimportant everyday issue. All of us who had close dealings with her knew that when we were going to talk with Haydée we had to be very clear as to what we were going to say, to have our ideas very well defined, very definite. If there was a weak element, if one aspect wasn't clear, she instantly questioned it; it never passed her by. I observed this many times. And she didn't do it with any intention of wounding or attacking but in order to exercise an elevated principle of truth and justice. When Haydée was convinced of something, she didn't believe in the word impossible, she was certain that everything could be sorted out; and because of that she was untiring, prepared to fight constantly. In contrast, she was a woman in whom one sensed a great interior pain, even when she was happy.

She was very Cuban. When she spoke, this was something that always stood out. Always, consciously or unconsciously, she was speaking of the essence of what it is to be Cuban. Haydée was very close to us, very close to the National Ballet of Cuba. Every time we had an important engagement or an event related to my artistic career, Haydée would appear. Suddenly, during a rehearsal in the darkness of a little corner of the empty theater we would discover that she was there watching us work. Or, lost among the public, looking on at a part of the performance. I never felt time passing between us; even though months would go by without our meeting I was aware that, even at a distance, she was in tune with what we were doing, and at any point would visit or write a letter or just a note: "I have been following every-thing. I haven't seen you, but I have felt you," she wrote me once. She was always concerned that we felt her support for our work, that we could count on her. And moreover, there was such a concern for me, personally, so spontaneous and natural in her. Whenever we met, even if there were many people present, she would come to me and place me at her side. I cannot remember ever having been in an event or meeting without Haydée being there at my side, because she always took me under her wing. There was always that delicacy, that simplicity of manner that was so intelligent and so beautiful. She always had a gesture for me, a kind word. I have kept one letter — I think it was the last one I received from her — in which instead of talking about "battling against everything for truth in art," she gave me one of the most emotional and overwhelming tributes that I have ever received. She talked of what "those I loved so much and are no longer here" saw in me. And she concluded: "You don't know, but today I am telling you, I have been your friend for many years." That was something that I didn't know, and that I will never forget.

For me, Haydée was really a very special woman. And when I hear talk of the importance of women being part of the struggle, in all the tasks, when it is affirmed that the success of a revolution greatly depends on the participation of women, I realize that women of her caliber are the ones who sow that force, the ones who teach the initial steps.

Haydée Under The Vines

Volodia Teitelboim

Chilean poet, essayist, journalist and novelist, Volodia Teitelboim has been called one of the most outstanding authors in both Chile and 20th century Latin America. In 2002 he was awarded the Chilean National Prize for Literature. He is well known for his profound humanism and his close identification with the history of the Chilean people.

As in the case of certain loves born of letters, I knew her first through a photograph.

My first memory is of a fuzzy photo. Her round face is a complete question. Her darkened blonde hair a wavy thicket. A lock falls over the middle of her forehead, over the meeting of her eyebrows, separating the half-closed eyes. There is a sense of astonishment in her large teeth. That old newspaper image is like a definition: the young woman is scanning a distant point as if unraveling the future. The sun filtering through the branches illuminates the right side of her well-worn khaki fatigues. The half-open jacket reveals an unwashed striped shirt; it is the poverty of multimillionaire souls.

She is not afraid, although above her head one can make out a horizontal rifle. A man, whose shoulder she does not reach and who has a cigar lodged in one side of his mouth, is pointing at a distant target. It is Fidel in the Sierra. And she is not only Abel's sister, but also that of Fidel and of Che. She is the woman who had a dream and wanted to fulfill it even at the cost of her life. She is Haydée.

For me, at that time she was already the legendary Haydée, a known unknown, unreachable.

Shortly after the Cuban Revolution, at the beginning of the Chilean fall, she traveled to Santiago de Chile. It was night when she arrived in the company of other Cubans at the house of a friend in the Ñuñoa district. That is when I witnessed the grapevine scene: Haydée immediately discovered the black grapes hanging in heavy clusters. She became ecstatic. Full of enthusiasm she reached up, stretching out her arms. She wanted to touch them. She was talking to herself. She cried out with contentment. She was like a child in a trance. She was born in a sugar mill in the province of Las Villas and had never seen anything like it. All the fruits of the tropical zone were there in the little town of Encrucijada, but never those dark blue grapes. I was dazzled by the spontaneous Dionysian gesture, that capacity for amazement as another way of loving life, of being surprised at something new. She was celebrating something more than a cult of fear. I already knew she was a heroine, a force within humanity, and I saw her adoring nature like a beautiful primitive being. Then I thought: in addition to courage, to love of the revolution, she has other gifts. In her voice full of exclamation there was a tender vibration. I felt I was beginning to know her.

After a political event in [Cuba's] Oriente province, we returned to the capital by plane. In the air, the mother of all storms caught us. Haydée continued talking as if she was in the lobby of the Riviera Hotel. She talked of her childhood, of her family. She created an atmosphere, a feeling of intimacy.

Good luck had it that she was in charge of looking after me when I attended the First Congress of the Communist Party of Cuba in December 1975. There was a meal with red candles. That woman made my imagination wander. She always established a correlation between the revolution and life. In her mouth nothing was ever rote. Everything was testimonial, action, moral value. I seemed to note in her regard a certain mysterious complexity. She had something of the visionary in her.

There are scars that are not visible. There are faces that hold a memory. She whispered as if searching within herself. She talked to me sadly of Violeta Parra. There was something in Violeta that attracted Haydée. Her singing, her poetry, her "thanks to life." Suddenly there was a return to splendor: with a smile of sweet pride she told me that the Casa de las Américas had the tapestries Violeta had exhibited in the Louvre. She confided in a more intimate tone: Violeta had her sympathy, as one of those people who do something beautiful for the good of the people.

Her voice became stronger. Now she was once more the conversationalist of the marvelous colloquium: here was Haydée talking of her daughter — Casa. Yes, that woman had a project as large as a continent. Apart from her children, she wanted to have a child of Cuba, who would be called Casa. The idea came to her in 1959, during the initial days of the blockade. In truth, she was in love with her America, with Martí's Our America, made incommunicado [by the blockade] by more than 20 walls, more impenetrable, more prohibitive than all the Andes. Those walls would have to be breached. The house Bolívar of dreamed would have to be united. Its soul had to be given flight, from the northern limit of Mexico to the confines of Cape Horn.

That could not be done without the weapons of the spirit. She put her hands to the task. She had a kind of magnetism to attract the horizons. She was often immersed in a soliloquy of questions and answers. There is Casa, "this tiny little place... in Havana," which today is the strongest tie of unity existing among all the cultures of our Latin America and the Caribbean.

Later I saw her again in the [Communist] Party Hotel in Moscow, when she was among carrying out tasks with one of her daughters. Once she said, "joy and sorrow are very closely linked." She had been in a car accident. Perhaps she was in shock.

Perhaps there are certain insoluble, indecipherable secrets, when a shadow of neurosis falls over the kingdom of transparency.

I saw her once more at the hotel. And then she left. But as a recollection she had left me some Cuban cheese, aromatic, succulent, as if saying to me: "Have a good breakfast. Everything is OK." I remembered her discovery of the black grapes, 20 years previously, under the vines, of that Santiago enfolded in fall... I would always see her that way, like an enchanted child, whatever the circumstance.

Then something very grave occurred. I didn't see her again. We received the news with shock. But she was not lost like a boat in the mist. She is made of the luminous material of life. The volcano that is Haydée never sleeps.

I have rarely met anyone more generous in her attitude toward the world, or more anxious to work for justice and truth. She was a pure woman in the most demanding sense, a person without protocol, full of an interior fire. All temperament and essential decency, she personified an impassioned revolution, a style that was born and died with her. Haydée is someone who did not die with her death. Neither did the revolution. Because both of them belong to the continuity of seeds. They were sown in what they did.

In a perfect poem, Fina García Marruz asks us to:

> Whisper to her than everything has been a dream.
> Pay her homage like a valient warrior
> Who lost only her last battle.

But the evidence remains that Haydée won the war.

Now There Is Only Life

Cintio Vitier

Cuban poet and essayist, Vitier presides over the Center for the Study of José Martí. He has served as professor at the Havana Normal School for Teachers and also at the Central University of Las Villas. He spent 15 years as a researcher at the José Martí National Library and has written various books of literary criticism of Martí's works. Married to the Cuban poet Fina García Marruz, Cintio Vitier won the Cuban National Prize for Literature in 1988 and was conferred the Juan Rulfo Prize in 2002.

I barely have recollections of Haydée, because I didn't have a lot to do with her and what we talked about only served to make me feel that we were not really talking; rather that I was guessing in the dark, and her in her blinding inclemency, creatures who loved each other and, for that reason, feared each other. I do retain a memory — or it retains me, and for that reason (because memory, in addition to recalling, knows) — I would say that there was an immense, almost explosive reserve of fear within her. I am not saying she was fearful, she never seemed to have been afraid, but a fear of love or a sacred fear, irascible in the face of the danger that always lies in wait for valor. It was as if she always saw valor (what one values and the valiant) as threatened, including in itself, in the very risk of its existing. Then her eyes would light up aggressively with love in the face of the imminent disaster of an intolerable injustice. She would maybe give advice, but most important was the indignant and supremely urgent look in her eyes, as if emerging from her heart to defend a child.

Because Haydée was really above everything a mother, a mother in permanent vigilance and attentiveness, who would not accept the diminution of those beings within her reach, under her protection. She practiced her love fiercely, with the total spontaneity of any genuine love. She did not even compromise with herself. And if at times she seemed pigheaded, it was out of the jealousy of love and a hunger for the truth and of what could be called — although it sounds abstract (or worse, pedantic) — absolute conviction. Conviction for her was unbending, it burned like the flaming bush in the desert, without being consumed by objects or people. It was, simply, the soul, or what only the soul sees. Words hardly ever satisfied her, they made her impatient, they pursued her impatiently, with the insistence of a pampered child, and all of a sudden she would seize, unexpectedly and glowing, the word.

When Haydée spoke of the Moncada attack, she did so as a participant not only in a historical event, but also in a biological and spiritual one. Like a mother talks of giving birth. The simile was hers and could only be hers because it was not a simile. Every time she talked about the Moncada (one of the most profound poetic events of the revolution), we felt ourselves to be present and awed at the bloody birth of an event greater than all of our memories. It could only be revealed again to her and to us by the apparition of a devastating detail or by the inflamed torrent of her words, a sleepless cry within, which threw up broken boulders, difficult to verbalize or utterly unspeakable.

Because it is also her voice, the rending and the tone, wounding as the wounded, of her voice flowing from a living source in front of the implacable judgment of her eyes. What those eyes confronted, face to face, was death. The eyes of a survivor, of a heroine, of a person brought back to life. Eyes flayed by death and resurrection. Haydée approached the death that remained to her for dying since the firing of the penultimate shot at

Moncada. Her death went with her, and through her. Her death was complete. Now it is simply life: her life and ours, of everything and everyone, inconsolable, untamed of hope.

February 1985

To Haydée, With All My Love

Alejandro Obregón

Colombian painter, muralist, sculptor and engraver, Alejandro Obregón's work has been exhibited throughout Latin America, Europe and the United States. Among his many awards are the Francisco Matarazzo Sobrinho Grand Prize for Latin America at the 9th Sao Paulo Biennial and first prize at the Gulf Caribbean Competition in Texas. His painting "Dead Student" (also known as "The Wake"), an allusion to the excesses of the dictatorship, won him the Guggenheim Prize for Colombia. His works are included in the collections of the Museo Nacional de Bogotá, the Museo de Arte Moderno de Bogotá, the Museum of Modern Art in New York, the Museo de Arte Moderno in Madrid, and the Museo Nacional de La Paz, among others. Alejandro Obregón died in 1992.

I got to know Haydée in Havana in 1977, when I traveled with Feliza Burztin and other artist colleagues to participate in a collective exhibition organized by the Casa de las Américas. On that occasion I displayed the work "La Cabeza de Galun" ["Galun's Head"], a tribute to a popular Colombian hero. Haydée's strong personality confused me initially; I remember we went with Mariano Rodríguez to visit a colonial house which was being restored as an art gallery for Casa. Haydée ordered the paneling to be removed. For his part, Mariano thought that it should be left, as it constituted a valid testament of other eras.

Impertinently, I took Mariano's side, among other reasons because houses live longer than people do and thus houses should recall people and not the other way around. Haydée looked at me with a certain mistrust. I don't know what happened to the paneling; but on account of it, our affection for each other was not instant. Other encounters followed that were marvelous and little by little I came to know her history as a heroine and her depth in seeing everything through a very special lens that was very much her own. By the end of my stay, she had my complete confidence and all my love.

I decided to paint a portrait of Haydée as a testimony of my affection for and admiration of her. I couldn't do it in the form of a painting that would reveal her image, but instead it came to me as a bunch of flowers that seemed like multiple portraits of Haydée's different facets — especially the middle one, a white flower — that for me was the soul of that great, terrible and tender woman, whose soul became blank again when she received the blue eyes of her brother Abel in her hands.

On a second trip I made to Havana and the first time we met up, just in passing, at Casa, I told her: "I didn't do a portrait of you, but I painted you some flowers." She responded with total frankness: "Obregón, I don't like painted flowers." "You'll see," I thought privately.

One or two days later we met up again and she rushed up to me saying: "Oh man, what a marvel of flowers you have painted. That white one, how wonderful!" I was happy because I knew she had recognized herself in them, and I also knew that she was beginning to love me through my painting. For me that was a great achievement, because one's painting has to be much better than oneself.

It's acceptable that as men we have to die. But not women. They should never die, and when they do one feels anger and takes it as a personal or even a collective offense. You, Haydée, and you, Feliza, who like all women of talent possessed that combination of being implacable and like little girls lost in the wood, have no right to die.

Big Sister

Ariel Dorfman

Chilean writer and left-wing intellectual who established himself as a novelist, poet, playwright and critic. A professor at the University of Chile, Dorfman was exiled for 10 years when his first novel, Moros en la costa *(published in English as* Hard Rain, *1990) came out just as the dictator Pinochet came to power in 1973. He continued to write fiction and poetry that addressed the coup while living in Europe and the United States. Currently a professor at Duke University in North Carolina, his critically acclaimed novels and books of poetry include* The Last Song of Manuel Sendero *(1987),* Last Waltz in Santiago *and* Other Poems of Exile and Disappearance *(1988). His play,* Death and the Maiden *(1991) was adapted for film in 1994.*

It is always difficult to recall the dead, and rather than erasing them, managing to make then more real as the years go by. And more so if they were already a legend when they were alive, like Haydée Santamaría.

For that reason, and so that she persists for others and persists for me, I would like to select just one of the moments in which I continue to feel her presence: when her eyes lit up despite her sorrow on that day when she received us in the Casa de las Américas a few months after the overthrow of Salvador Allende. I had come, resisting and defeated, from Chile, and that woman who had seen so many deaths in the peoples' causes, as well as some victories and resurrections, opened her arms to welcome me and give me strength. How good it would have been to receive her at some point in a free and democratic Chile and, as a welcoming gift, show her a people without fear and without hunger. As that is no longer possible, the only thing that remains for me is to promise that when that day arrives, in the celebrations I will remember the solidarity of my big sister, which was also the affection of Cuba and the ever-present company of Casa, our Haydée.

Washington, February 1985

Haydée Invented Happiness

Carmen Naranjo

Born in Costa Rica, Carmen Naranjo deals with the economic, political and social issues which beset Central America in her novels which include: Memorias de un hombre de palabra *(1968),* Responso por el niño Juan Manuel *(1971) and* Sobrepunto *(1985). In her most famous novel,* El Diario de una multitud *(1974), she attempts to discover solutions for an unjust and cruel society. Naranjo is also a well-known poet whose collections include:* Homenaje a don Nadie *(1981) and* Mi guerrilla *(1984).*

From very early on, Haydée Santamaría was castigated by pain: the loss of Abel, the death of her fiancé, her precarious health. This great Cuban woman, however, dealt with it in such a way that she seemingly invented happiness. I am unable to remember her without her open and cordial smile.

Haydée, with her work at the Casa de la Américas, fulfilled in the field of art and literature the cause of Simón Bolívar and José Martí: Latin American unity. Casa was and is the center for writers and artists, the link between closed borders and permanently isolated countries, the opportunity to know and read of each other, a stimulus to create an encounter with that boundless Cuban generosity.

Those of us who arrived as jurists for the Casa de las Américas prizes encountered a smiling and joking Haydée who woke us up at night in disguise first to scare us and then to have a great laugh at us.

The joy she invented was so intense that it still pains me to recall that I will never again find her in that beautiful city, Havana.

There Where The Light Does Not Forget Its Warriors

Fina García Marruz

On the death of a national heroine
Place a leaf on the forehead of suicide.
An evergreen in the dip of her neck.
Cover her with flowers: Ophelia.
Those who loved her have been orphaned.
Cover her with the tenderness of tears.
Become the dew that refreshes her sorrow.
And if the piety of flowers does not suffice
Whisper to her that everything has been a dream.
Pay her homage like a valiant warrior
Who lost only her last battle.
Let her not be alone in her inconsolable hour.
Her deeds, let them not be forgotten in the grass.
Let them be picked, one by one,
There where the light does not forget its warriors.

August 1980

To the Casa de las Américas

Roberto Matta

Chilean painter, printmaker and draughtsman, Roberto Matta was one of the few Surrealist artists to take on political, social and spiritual themes directly. In his youth as a merchant marine he traveled to Europe where he met famous architects Lecorbusier and Alvar Aalto, the poet Federico García Lorca, and the artists Salvador Dalí, Andre Breton and Marcel Duchamp. Matta visited Cuba in the 1960s to work with art students. He died in 2002.

To Casa de las Américas
With love and with reason, my love
for Haydée finds no wrong in the
reasoning of her heart.
Because individual reason does not know
the shared reasoning of the heart.

Because the shared reason is a common reason
and each one of us ourselves, is that other
in the shared reason of a heart.
With my most complete love
for the life of Haydée.

To Haydée

Ernesto Che Guevara

Dear Yeyé:

Armando and Guillermo told me of your tribulations. I respect your decision and I understand it, but I would have liked to have embraced you in person rather than through this epistle. The security regulations during my stay here have been very severe and that has deprived me of seeing many people whom I love (I am not as cold as I sometimes appear). These days I come to Cuba almost like a foreigner on a visit; I look at everything from a different angle. And the impression, despite my isolation, makes me understand the impression that visitors take with them.

Thanks for the medicinal-literary dispatches. I see that you have become a *literati* with the power of creation, but I will confess that how I most like you is on that day in the New Year, with all of your fuses blown and firing cannons on all sides. That image, and that of the Sierra — even our fights in those days are pleasant memories — are what I will carry of you for my own use. The affection and decisiveness of all of you will help us in the difficult times ahead.

Love,

Your colleague

Closer to Haydée Santamaría and the Casa de las Américas

Fidel Castro

Commander in Chief of the Cuban Rebel Army, Fidel Castro and his July 26 Movement combatants defeated the dictatorship of Fulgencio Batista on January 1, 1959. Haydée and her brother Abel worked closely with him to plan the July 26, 1953 attack on the Moncada Garrison which began the revolutionary struggle. A trusted compañera, *political and cultural adviser, Haydée was never far from Fidel's side. This excerpt is from a speech given at the opening of the Haydée Santamaría Printing Complex in Santiago de Cuba on December 27, 1983.*

Haydée has a really beautiful revolutionary history. It began with the founding of the July 26 Movement, when Abel joined the movement and she, too, participated from the beginning, playing an exceptional role. In the whole of the preparations for the July 26, 1953, attack, Haydée — a hardworking, untiring, very modest *compañera* — devoted herself totally to the revolutionary cause. She was an extraordinary help and acted brilliantly, displaying an exceptional value not only in transporting weapons (and in the days leading up to July 26 it was she who had to carry guns and bullets in suitcases, under cover) but also in the Moncada days. In the days following the Moncada assault, working underground on the organization of the Movement, in the November 30 uprising once again underground, in the Sierra Maestra and in the revolution. Yeyé's name is essentially linked to the Cuban Revolution's prestige in Cuba and Latin America. I have to say that the work she undertook in many fields, but above all as the head of the Casa de la Américas, has had exceptional repercussions in the field of Latin American culture and literature. Today, the Casa de las Américas is the most prestigious institution of its kind on our continent. Moreover, it has international prestige beyond the continent. Latin America's most significant literary figures have in one way or another participated in events at the Casa de las Américas. Many of them knew Yeyé, and all those who knew her speak of her with great respect. That institution also developed the work of the revolution: the goals of the revolution and the revolution's literary and cultural labors. And our comrade Haydée Santamaría dedicated her finest efforts to that task. For that reason it is completely logical, appropriate and just that an institution such as this, which produces things as valuable as books, which is called upon to have such significance in our people's educational and cultural development, should bear the honorable and glorious name of Haydée Santamaría.

Notes for a Song to Yeyé

Silvio Rodríguez

Cuban singer, guitar player and composer, Silvio Rodríguez is one of the most respected troubadours of Latin America. In 1967, together with Pablo Milanés and Noel Nicola, he founded the Nueva Trova [New Song] movement, which today has more than 300 musician members. His first album, "Días y Flores," appeared in 1976, and he has since composed more than 500 songs. His unique combination of lyrical poetry and poignant political commentary has made him a musical legend in Cuba and throughout Latin America.

Anyone who might ask why the Casa de las Américas opened its doors to us in February 1968 should be aware that the gesture did not come out of a void, and less still on account of promising news of the young singer-songwriters. At that time we were usually preceded by the epithet "*conflictivos*" (troublemakers), a word used as a synonym for "watch out for them." Perhaps for that reason, before we were invited to sing, Haydée Santamaría met with us personally to get a sense of our understanding of universal and domestic issues as well as our backgrounds and travels.

What determined that initial interest? Somebody said that the first person to talk about our group of singers was the documentary filmmaker Santiago Alvarez. I believe this because I knew Santiago. What was the initial communication with Haydée about? It might seem strange but to a certain extent it was about our repertoire. Strange, because we arrived under the auspices of the Protest Song Center and our arsenal of such songs was not prodigious. In other words, when we came face to face with Haydée, we had not written much at all on themes like the war in Vietnam, racial discrimination and anti-imperialism. For his part, the revolutionary singer of the time was — and always will be — Carlos Puebla. We were something else from the beginning. We fused everyday events with transcendental ones and did not avoid speaking out on the setbacks of the society in revolution. We sang like that because our life was like that, and real life usually puts the best words into song. This wasn't a conflict for Haydée, who always listened to us respectfully, whatever we sang. Just once she asked me what I wanted to say when I wrote: "I will go to sing to the thunder / of an unknown country." It was then when, forced to elaborate, I confided in her my secret aspiration to become an internationalist combatant.

Perhaps the subject that prompted our closest affinity was Che and the armed struggle. She liked to talk of when they became friends in the Sierra Maestra and I loved to listen to her, silently lamenting not having been old enough to be part of that uprising. In the Sierra he had promised her that she would be with him at the hour of Latin American liberation (the spark would fade a little when she explained why they hadn't been able to share that destiny). More than once she also told me that the Argentine would say that what he most liked about her was to see her "firing cannons on all sides," like a rebel in the heart of the rebels. I suppose that must have been another fundamental point of our identity: the conviction that it was necessary to go on being insurrectionists, so as to give continuity to the finest revolutionary spirit. By historic right, she was a sister spirit of Che. By vocation and age, I was a slave of Martínez Villena (the Giant). With such a special identity in common, we quickly became friends.

As I have already said, Haydée placed the revolutionary epic within our reach, by recounting some of the events as she recalled them and not as they would seem to have been painted by a certain castrating mythology. Her poetic and, at the same time, realistic vision was the declaration that sacrifice was a way of ascending the human scale. Thus, feeling steadily more committed, although without ties, we came to be like sister and brother and she ceased to be Haydée and became Yeyé, as she was called by Doña Joaquina and her sisters Aida and Adita, who also became like family.

It could be that I am a little more cautious now than I was in those days, when everything — including myself — was much younger. At that time, although my spirit sometimes went too far, failing to confront contradictions seemed to me to be cowardice and, not being impetuous, a defect. Haydée had a tremendous capacity for comprehension and compassion in the face of those flights. She knew where it is written and how to read why everyone is how everyone is. The pain in her soul, the tragic aspects of her life, refined her tenderness to the sublime. At the same time she was able to sit down and discuss things with anyone and to speak a few home truths. And, marvelously, she also possessed the admirable habit of not adding fuel to the flames. If someone went off about a comrade, or something of the sort, Haydée would not allow any ill-speaking, quite the reverse. Thus, when you heard her repeatedly insisting on someone's virtues, you knew that for some reason that person had been put in the funeral chapel, so to speak. She was like a great academic of humanity in a little body and with the voice of a flute. But nobody could be mistaken about the character that resided within that being, who spoke as though she were singing. For me, Yeyé was the mortar that bound those shapeless things still dancing within me.

I will never forget that when *trova* singers Vicente Feliú, Lázaro García, Augusto Blanca and Saresquita Escalona were kidnapped and tortured during a coup d'état in Bolivia, Yeyé transformed her office in the Casa de las Américas into an international mobilization center. From there she planned and executed their rescue and never rested until she knew that they were on their way home.

The fascination she had for me led me to write hundreds of words with music, with which I dedicated a tribute to the prowess of her generation, among which her brother Abel shone out. In other words, if our friendship hadn't existed it is possible that I would never have written certain songs, like "Canción del Elegido" ("Song of the Chosen One"). During the years that we knew each other, I managed to get her to sign my copy of the book *Haydée Habla del Moncada* (Haydée Speaks on the Moncada), where she wrote: "Silvio, understand me and love me." Those could be the key words for the song that I owe her. As you can see, I am trying to transcribe something of her memory in ordinary language, without being able to reveal the magnitude of her presence.

I mustn't forget to say that we also laughed a lot with her. She loved to laugh and make others laugh. If you believe that the senses are an attribute of personality, one of the essential ones in Yeyé was that of humor, at times endowed by her expansive maternal feeling. I remember that one day she invited me to eat, and while the rest of the diners were served a Cuban dish, she placed in front of me an unusual omelet made with ripe plantain. That was because she once heard me say that I liked that dish very much.

One December 31, the date she had chosen for her birthday, I saw her whiten her face with powder, throw a sheet over her head and illuminate her chin with a lantern. After turning out all the lights, she appeared like that in front of a *compañero* who was snoring on a sofa. He leapt up fuming and swearing, and the next day was mortified at the words that had escaped from his mouth. Whenever Haydée saw him after that, she would dig him in the ribs with a finger and giggle.

The last time Julio Cortázar was in Cuba, we had breakfast together. We had bumped into each other at some event, but seeking a further conversation, agreed to meet up early one Sunday in the Riviera Hotel. While we were going there, Haydée, who was also to be at the breakfast, explained the situation to me: Cortázar had a new girlfriend, and wanted to show her Havana. Initially, so that he could move about freely during his visit, he had been offered a vehicle and driver, but Julio, *cronopio* par excellence and thus an enemy of causing the least inconvenience, had declined the car and had asked for a couple of bicycles to tour the city.

"So, Silvio, at some point during breakfast, you have to say that you have no way to get to your activities and need a bicycle," the heroine of Moncada instructed me as she drove along the Malecón.

"And why should I do that, Yeyé?"

"To see what Julio says, man." And she looked at me with those brilliant eyes.

Fool that I was, I spent the breakfast ignoring Yeyé's nudges, delaying what we had agreed. I was in conflict, because on the one hand I felt for Julio's frankness and on the other I didn't want to let down my accomplice by not playing my part. To summarize the story: when I finally managed to say that I needed a bicycle, Julio reacted with his proverbial generosity, saying that he hap- pened to have two and he'd be delighted to lend me one. That moment was the blossoming of the morning: Yeyé exploding with laughter, my tomato face and Cortázar's expression, at first disconcerted and trying to come to an understanding, until he finally arched his eyebrows and began to shake his head on hearing our friend say:

"Get that, Julio! With the scarcity of bicycles that we have...!"

radical history ▮

a new series from Ocean Press

CHILE: THE OTHER SEPTEMBER 11 ▮

Commentaries and Reflections on the 1973 Coup in Chile
Edited by Pilar Aguilera and Ricardo Fredes

An anthology reclaiming the day of September 11 as the anniversary
of the U.S.-backed coup in Chile by General Augusto Pinochet,
against the popularly elected government of Salvador Allende.

Contributors include:
Ariel Dorfman: *The Last September 11*
Pablo Neruda: *I Begin By Invoking Walt Whitman*
President Salvador Allende: *Last Words*
Joan Jara: *The Coup, Unfinished Song*
Victor Jara: *Estadio Chile*
Beatriz Allende: *We Never Saw Him Hesitate*
Fidel Castro: *On the Coup in Chile*

ISBN 1-876175-50-8

Published in Spanish as:
CHILE: EL OTRO 11 DE SEPTIEMBRE (ISBN 1-876175-72-9)

ONE HUNDRED RED HOT YEARS ▮

Big Moments of the 20th Century
Edited by Deborah Shnookal
Preface by Eduardo Galeano

A thrilling ride through the 20th Century — 100 years of revolution,
reaction and resistance.
ISBN 1-876175-48-6

POLITICS ON TRIAL

Five Famous Trials of the 20th Century

William Kunstler

Introduction by Michael Ratner, Karin Kunstler and Michael Smith

As the United States once again finds itself adrift in a violent sea of patriotism, bigotry and fear, it is an appropriate time to address this country's dark past of political repression and racist scapegoating. William Kunstler, champion of civil liberties and human rights, reflects on five famous examples in which ordinary citizens were targeted for the color of their skin or the views they held. The introduction assesses new threats to civil liberties posed by the "war on terrorism."

Includes essays on:

Bartolomeo Vanzetti and Nicola Sacco

Scopes: The "Monkey Trial"

The Scottsboro Nine

The Rosenbergs

Engel, Education and God

ISBN 1-876175-49-4

rebel lives

helen keller
edited by John Davis

"I have entered the fight against the economic system in which we live. It is to be a fight to the finish and I ask no quarter."
— Helen Keller

Poor little blind girl or dangerous radical? This book challenges the sanitized image of Helen Keller, restoring her true history as a militant socialist. Here are her views on women's suffrage, her defense of the Industrial Workers of the World (IWW), her opposition to World War I and her support for imprisoned socialist and anarchist leaders, as well as her analysis of disability and class.

ISBN 1-876175-60-5

albert einstein
edited by Jim Green

"What I like most about Albert Einstein is that he was a troublemaker." — Fred Jerome, author of *The Einstein File*

You don't have to be Einstein... to know that he was a giant in the world of science and physics. Yet this book takes a new, subversive look at *Time* magazine's "Person of the Century," whose passionate opposition to war and racism and advocacy of human rights put him on the FBI's files as a socialist enemy of the state.

ISBN 1-876175-63-X

oceanpress

e-mail info@oceanbooks.com.au
www.oceanbooks.com.au